Beginner's *Baking* — BIBLE —

Beginner's *Baking* BIBLE

130+ Recipes and Techniques for New Bakers

Heather Perine

PHOTOGRAPHY BY HELENE DUJARDIN

callisto
publishing
an imprint of Sourcebooks

Copyright © 2019 by Callisto Publishing LLC
Cover and internal design © 2019 by Callisto Publishing LLC
Photography © 2019 Helene Dujardin. Food styling by Anna Hampton.
Author photo courtesy of © Emily Brenchley, www.emilybrenchleyphotography.com
Interior and Cover Designer: Stephanie Mautone
Art Producer: Michael Hardgrove
Editor: Jesse Aylen
Production Editor: Chris Gage

Published by Callisto Publishing LLC C/O Sourcebooks LLC
P.O. Box 4410, Naperville, Illinois 60567-4410
(630) 961-3900
callistopublishing.com

Printed in the United States of America
VP 2

To Jason, for tasting all the treats
(good and bad) and for washing all those dishes.
Without you, this book would never
have been possible. And to my mom,
for being my biggest cheerleader.

Red Velvet Layer Cake **PAGE 134**

Contents

Introduction

When it comes to being in the kitchen, I don't think there is anything more rewarding than baking something from scratch. Baking for someone is the best way I know of to show them I care. We celebrate milestones in our lives—from birthdays to anniversaries—with baked goods or share them to let someone know we are thinking about them. However, as inspiring as baking can be, it can also be intimidating. One thing that seems to scare people away is a fear of having to closely follow a recipe. In cooking, you can throw in a pinch of this or that without a fear of failure. But baking requires reading a recipe, using precise measurements, and applying specific techniques. And, yes, failure can happen. Cookies can fall flat. Cakes can sink. Sometimes breads won't rise. But that's okay, and baking doesn't have to be scary. Baking is a science, after all. Once you get the basics down, you will have eliminated the guesswork and it will be sweet (or savory) success every time.

Growing up, my only baking experience was making the classic cookie recipe we all know from that yellow bag of chocolate chips. I don't come from a long line of chefs, and I haven't attended culinary school; I'm a home baker just like you. I took up—and fell in love with—baking in my early twenties when I took a culinary class. After that, I wanted to learn as much as possible. I read every cookbook I could get my hands on and took every course I could find. The best teacher, however, was simply practicing—and sometimes failing—in my own kitchen. And that's how I know that learning to become a better baker is something anyone can do.

In the *Beginner's Baking Bible*, you will learn how to make an assortment of baked goods that will impress your friends and family, including classic breakfast staples like blueberry muffins and buttermilk biscuits, as well as cookies, cakes, pies, tarts, quiches, and even savory breads. In addition to the recipes themselves, I'll share my best tips and tricks that I've learned through my own missteps, and help you troubleshoot recipes so you can grow your skills as a baker. Baking is something that can be easily learned. You don't need a culinary degree or a "baking gene" to be successful. The best way to learn is by simply getting started.

So, are you ready? Let's get baking!

PART I

The Beginner's Building Blocks

1

The Beginning Baker's Kitchen

*T*o bake a range of delicious confections, you don't need to use fancy gadgets, obscure processes, or hard-to-find ingredients. You will need some basics to get the job done properly, however. In this chapter, I'll share must-have tools and ingredients to stock your kitchen, plus the nice-to-have items for when you're ready to move beyond the basics.

ESSENTIAL EQUIPMENT

It can be tempting to stock your kitchen with every single pan and appliance available—trust me, I know! But, as I've learned over the years, you need only a few essential items to tackle most baking recipes.

Cookware and Bakeware

MUST HAVE

Baking sheets: Flat metal baking sheets are available with a rim or without. I prefer ones with a rim because they can be used to bake cookies, bars, and even cakes. Invest in two so you can rotate batches in and out of the oven.

Baking pans: Baking pans come in a variety of sizes and shapes—most have sides about 2 inches deep. My go-to baking pans are a 9-by-13-inch rectangular pan, an 8-by-8-inch square pan, 8½-by-4½-inch and 9-by-5-inch loaf pans, two 9-inch round cake pans, and a 12-cup cupcake/muffin pan. I recommend aluminum baking pans for their even heating and cooling properties.

Pie dish: I recommend a 9-inch glass pie dish.

NICE TO HAVE

Bundt cake pan: A Bundt pan is a round metal pan with a hole in the middle and uniform ridges up the side.

Tart pan: This 9- or 10-inch round pan has fluted edges and a removable bottom, making it ideal for baking beautiful tarts.

Tools and Utensils

MUST HAVE

Measuring tools: Invest in a set of dry measuring cups, a glass liquid measuring cup, and a set of measuring spoons. Choose metal and glass, as plastic can retain odors and residue.

Mixing tools: A set of mixing bowls (again, metal is best), a silicone spatula, and a wire whisk are essential.

Cooling rack: Baked goods continue to bake once you've removed them from the oven. Proper cooling on a wire rack helps ensure that they don't end up overbaked.

Rolling pin: A wooden rolling pin is essential for pie dough, certain types of cookies, and breads. My favorite is a French rolling pin made of solid wood that is tapered at the ends.

Parchment paper or silicone baking mat: Parchment paper or a reusable silicone baking mat makes cleanup a breeze and keeps cookies from spreading too much.

NICE TO HAVE

Cookie scoop: A cookie scoop ensures that you have evenly sized cookies every time.

Microplane rasp grater: A rasp grater makes zesting citrus and grating fresh nutmeg quick and easy.

Appliances

MUST HAVE

Mixer: Handheld electric mixers with beaters are available in a range of price points and make fast work of creaming butter and sugar for cookies, mixing cake batters, and whipping egg whites.

NICE TO HAVE

Food processor: This makes quick work of assembling pie dough, chopping nuts, and shredding vegetables (like carrots for a carrot cake).

Stand mixer: If you have space in your kitchen and your budget, a stand mixer is a great investment. Thanks to its large capacity and heavy-duty motor, making cakes and cookie dough, whipping egg whites, and kneading bread dough become fast and easy tasks.

ESSENTIAL INGREDIENTS

Just like you don't need fancy equipment to be successful, you don't need exotic or expensive ingredients either. It is important, however, to use quality ingredients. Any of these staple ingredients can easily be found at your local grocery store.

MUST HAVE

Flours: Flour builds structure because it contains proteins that, when hydrated, form gluten. Without gluten, your baked goods would fall apart. All-purpose flour has moderate protein content, making it ideal for many recipes. Bread flour has higher protein content, which gives bread its elasticity. Cake flour has lower protein content, which gives cakes a delicate texture. Store flour in a cool, dry place.

Sugars: Best known as a sweetener, sugar also provides moisture. The most commonly used sugars are granulated white, brown (light or dark), and powdered (confectioner's). Use caution when substituting sugar alternatives, such as honey, because they can affect texture. Store sugar in a cool, dry place.

Fats: Fats are crucial in making baked goods tender and moist and, depending on which type you use, can also add flavor.

Butter (salted and unsalted): Butter is wonderful to use for baking because it provides great flavor. I recommend unsalted butter, partly because the amount of salt in salted butter can vary among brands. If you do opt for salted butter, mindfully reduce the amount of salt in the recipe. Store butter, wrapped, in your refrigerator.

Shortening: Shortening is pure fat and increases the tenderness of baked goods, though it doesn't provide the flavor that butter does. Store shortening on your pantry shelf.

Alternatives: Many recipes call for oil instead of butter or shortening. I recommend using a neutral-tasting oil, such as vegetable or canola oil. Other fats such as lard, coconut oil, or margarine can also be used.

Leavening agents: Leavening agents are what cause your baked goods to rise. There are three different kinds: chemical (baking powder or baking soda), biological (yeast), or physical (air or steam). Chemical and biological leavening agents can expire over time, so test them for a reaction before you start (read ahead to find out how).

Baking powder: They may sound similar, but baking powder and baking soda are not interchangeable. Baking powder is baking soda that's been mixed with an acid. Most baking powders are double acting, meaning they react once when moistened and again when heat is applied. Test baking powder by dropping a bit of hot water into a small spoonful to see if it bubbles.

Baking soda: Baking soda, or bicarbonate of soda, reacts with a recipe's acidic ingredients, such as buttermilk, though it can be used on its own to help leaven a recipe. Before you use that ancient box of baking soda lurking in the cupboard, test it with a drop of vinegar or lemon juice to see if it still bubbles.

Yeast: A must-have ingredient when making bread, yeast is a living organism that eats sugar and releases carbon dioxide. When activating yeast, always use warm liquids (105°F to 110°F). Hot liquids will kill it, and cold liquids will not activate it. Opened packets of yeast should be stored in the refrigerator and used by their expiration date.

NICE TO HAVE

Chocolate: Chocolate comes in many forms and contains varying amounts of sugar. For bars and baking chocolate, the higher the percentage of cocoa, the less sugar it has. So an 80 percent chocolate bar is less sweet than a 60 percent chocolate bar. I use unsweetened cocoa powder in these recipes. As Dutch-processed cocoa doesn't produce the same reaction, it should not be substituted. Chocolate should be stored in a cool, dry place.

Nuts: Nuts bring flavor and texture to many recipes. For added flavor, try roasting them before using. If they aren't in the budget, or if nut allergies are a concern, you can always omit them. Nuts are best stored in your freezer.

A Sense About Salt

Salt is essential in baking. It might seem strange to add salt to a dessert, but it helps enhance other flavors, balance sweetness, strengthen bread dough, and make your baked goods last longer. You may notice some recipes call for salt and others call for kosher salt. What's the difference? Regular salt, or table salt, has smaller granules. Kosher salt has larger granules and may not dissolve as easily. If a recipe calls for kosher salt and you add table salt, you may be adding more salt than the recipe calls for, which will result in oversalting. When a recipe simply calls for salt, use table salt.

PERFECT YOUR PROCESS

Anyone who knows me will tell you that organization is not my strong suit—until it's time to bake. Preparation is essential to making baking enjoyable, so here are my most valuable preparation techniques to help you perfect your process.

Prep it: The French call this *mise en place*, or "everything in its place." Read the recipe in its entirety and organize your ingredients before getting started. Allow butter and eggs to come to room temperature, prep your pans, preheat the oven, and prepare ingredients like roasted and chopped nuts. These steps ensure a smooth process and prevent a frantic rush to the store mid-bake for that one surprise missing ingredient!

Grease it: There's nothing worse than going through all the trouble of baking from scratch only to have your treats stick to the pan. Prepare your pans according to the recipe instructions (by coating them with cooking spray, butter, or butter and flour, or lining them with parchment paper or a silicone baking mat) before you start.

Measure it: Successful baking boils down to accurate measurement, which means using the right equipment for the right process. Although it might be tempting to measure your liquids in your dry measuring cups, you won't get an accurate measurement. Use your glass measuring cup and get down to eye level for the best read.

Separate it: Separating eggs is best done with cold eggs, because the yolk is firmer and less likely to break. Separate eggs one at a time in two small bowls. Crack the egg and transfer the egg back and forth gently between your hands, letting the egg white drip into one bowl. When there is no egg white left in your hand, place the egg yolk into the other bowl.

Mix it: It's tempting to throw everything in the bowl all at once to save a few minutes. Although that's probably how many of us baked when we kids, we know better now. Mix your dry ingredients and wet ingredients separately, then combine them together as directed in the recipe. Be careful not to overmix, which can cause certain baked goods to become tough.

Check it: I've taken my fair share of cakes out of the oven too early, only to have my heart sink just like the center of those cakes. Begin checking for doneness at the earliest listed cook time. To

The Measure Matters

To accurately measure flour, start by stirring up the flour in your container since flour can settle as it sits. Use a spoon to scoop the flour into your dry measuring cup. Do not pack the flour down or tap the sides when measuring, as this can result in using too much flour. Once you have a heaping cup, level it off with a flat edge, like the back of a knife.

When measuring sugar, there's a distinct difference between measuring granulated sugar and brown sugar. For granulated sugar, simply scoop it into the measuring cup and level off. Brown sugar, however, needs to be packed down to get an accurate measure. Using the back of a spoon, press down on the sugar until it is firmly packed into your measuring cup. When you have a heaping cupful, level it off.

test for doneness of cakes and cupcakes, insert a toothpick into the center and look for moist crumbs when you extract it. Every oven is different, so don't blindly trust the time listed: Use your eyes and your nose to judge when your baked good is ready.

Just cool it: Just because you took your baked goods out of the oven doesn't mean you're done. Because baked foods can continue to bake when left in the pan (due to residual heat), be sure to follow the recipe instructions and allow them to cool properly on a cooling rack.

2

Starting Skills

I'm going to let you in on a little secret: You have the potential to be a great baker. All it takes is knowing a few essential techniques and a little practice. In this chapter, I'll share the skills you'll use in this cookbook. By the end, you'll be ready to break out those mixing bowls, roll up your sleeves, and start baking with the best of them.

BAKING TECHNIQUES

Mastering key baking techniques—mixing, folding, creaming, kneading, melting, and more—is easier than you'd expect. Just follow these tips and instructions.

Mixing and Folding

Mixing means to stir the ingredients together until they are combined, and it can be done by hand or with an electric mixer. Folding means to combine the ingredients softly to avoid overmixing.

1. To fold lighter ingredients, such as whipped egg whites or whipped cream, into a denser mixture, such as a batter or a custard, add a small amount of the lighter ingredient to the denser mixture, then use a spatula to cut from side to side through the middle of the bowl.

2. Scrape the spatula toward you along the bottom of the bowl, then gently fold the mixture up over itself. Rotate the bowl and repeat this process until the ingredients are combined. Add the rest of the lighter ingredients and fold until they are fully incorporated.

Creaming Butter and Sugar

Creaming is the process of beating air into butter, which provides structure for baked goods. Sugar is responsible for "punching" holes in the butter and creating air pockets. Always use softened butter. Creaming can be done by hand or with a mixer.

1. Add the sugar to the butter.

2. Mix until the butter has a light color and fluffy texture. If using a mixer, set it at medium speed and mix for 2 to 3 minutes. Be careful to not to overmix, which can result in a dense finished product.

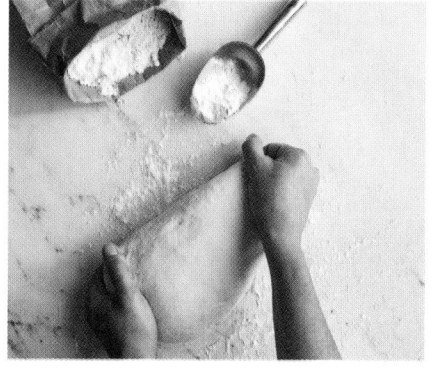

Kneading Dough

Kneading dough helps develop the gluten, which is responsible for the strength and structure of yeasted doughs. The steps here are for kneading by hand, but you can also use a stand mixer fitted with a dough hook attachment—just remember to use the "windowpane test" to check the dough's progress.

1. Shape the dough into a ball. Using the palms of your hands, push the dough down and away from your body.

2. Fold the dough in half, give it a quarter turn, and repeat step 1 until the dough is soft and supple (up to 10 minutes).

3. To check if the dough has been kneaded long enough, conduct the "windowpane test." Remove a piece of dough and stretch it into a thin membrane that you can see through. If the dough tears while stretching, knead it a bit more.

Whipping Egg Whites

Whipping egg whites adds air into the whites to lighten them into a fluffy cloud. Whipped egg whites can be used for meringues or to help cakes rise.

1. Start with clean, dry metal bowls and utensils. Separate the egg whites from the yolks, making sure there is no trace of yolk in the whites, as yolks can prevent the egg whites from whipping up fully.

2. Using an electric mixer, start mixing on low and gradually increase the speed to whip the egg whites to your desired firmness.

3. When the egg whites are properly whipped, soft peaks will hold their shape but will fall over when you lift the beaters from the bowl. Firm peaks will not fall over when you lift the beaters from the bowl.

Cutting Butter into Flour

"Cutting in" means to incorporate butter into flour. It is the key to making tender, flaky pastries, biscuits, and pie crusts. Unless otherwise stated in the recipe, always use cold butter, preferably cut into small cubes. If you don't have a pastry blender, you can also use a food processor for this task, but be sure to pulse the butter into the flour, so as not to overwork the dough.

1. Put the flour and butter into a bowl. Using a pastry blender, cut and blend the butter into the flour.

2. Continue blending until the butter is in pea-size pieces and the texture is pebbly, with small visible pieces of butter coated in flour.

Melting Chocolate

Melting chocolate can be done on the stovetop or in the microwave. Either way, be sure your utensils are completely dry. If water gets into the chocolate, the chocolate can seize.

1. To melt chocolate on the stove, place the chopped chocolate in a double boiler or a heat-proof bowl set over a pot of simmering water. Stir frequently.

2. To melt chocolate in the microwave, place the chocolate in a heat-proof bowl and heat in 30-second intervals. Stir between each interval to prevent burning.

PART II

The Recipes

Double Chocolate Chip Bread

Makes 1 (9-by-5-inch) loaf

You can enjoy this rich, fudgy bread any time of day, but I suggest serving it as a dessert alongside a cup of good, strong coffee. *Nut-free*

PREP TIME: 20 minutes
COOK TIME: 55 minutes

1½ cups all-purpose flour

½ cup unsweetened cocoa powder

½ teaspoon salt

½ teaspoon baking powder

½ teaspoon baking soda

½ cup vegetable oil

1 cup light brown sugar

2 large eggs, room temperature

1 cup buttermilk

1 cup semisweet chocolate chips, tossed with 1 tablespoon of flour

1. Preheat the oven. Preheat the oven to 350°F. Butter and flour a 9-by-5-inch loaf pan or lightly coat with cooking spray.

2. Combine the dry ingredients. In a medium bowl, whisk together the flour, cocoa powder, salt, baking powder, and baking soda.

3. Combine the wet ingredients. In a large bowl, combine the oil, sugar, eggs, and buttermilk.

4. Add the dry ingredients. Add the dry ingredients to the wet ingredients and mix together with a rubber spatula. Stir in the chocolate chips.

5. Bake. Pour the batter into the pan and bake for 50 to 55 minutes, or until a toothpick inserted into the center comes out clean. Set the pan on a wire rack and cool completely.

TOPPING TIP: Glaze the bread with Chocolate Ganache (page 171) and turn this into a triple chocolate bread!

Cinnamon Swirl Bread

Makes 1 (9-by-5-inch) loaf

I just can't resist anything that has a cinnamon swirl running through it, like this moist and comforting quick bread. *Nut-free*

PREP TIME: 20 minutes

COOK TIME: 55 minutes

FOR THE TOPPING

⅓ cup light brown sugar

2 teaspoons ground cinnamon

FOR THE BREAD

2 cups all-purpose flour

1 teaspoon baking soda

½ teaspoon salt

½ cup granulated sugar

½ cup light brown sugar

1 teaspoon vanilla extract

1 large egg, room temperature

1 cup buttermilk

¼ cup vegetable oil

TO MAKE THE TOPPING

Make the topping. In a small bowl, combine the brown sugar and cinnamon.

TO MAKE THE BREAD

1. Preheat the oven. Preheat the oven to 350°F. Butter and flour a 9-by-5-inch loaf pan or lightly coat with cooking spray.

2. Combine the dry ingredients. In a medium bowl, whisk together the flour, baking soda, and salt.

3. Combine the wet ingredients. In a second medium bowl, combine the granulated sugar, brown sugar, vanilla, egg, buttermilk, and oil.

4. Combine wet and dry ingredients. Add the dry ingredients to the wet ingredients and mix together with a rubber spatula.

5. Make the swirl. Pour half of the batter into pan. Sprinkle with half of the cinnamon and sugar mixture. Pour the remaining batter into the pan and top with the remaining cinnamon and sugar mixture. Draw a knife through batter, swirling in circles, to marble.

6. Bake. Pour the batter into the pan and bake for 50 to 55 minutes, or until a toothpick inserted into the center comes out clean. Set the pan on a wire rack and cool completely.

SUBSTITUTION TIP: If you don't have buttermilk, make your own. Combine 1 cup of milk with 1 tablespoon of lemon juice (or vinegar) and stir. Allow to sit for 10 minutes before using.

Red Velvet Layer Cake **PAGE 134**

7

Captivating Cakes and Cupcakes

Vanilla Cupcakes

Makes 12 cupcakes

I've made these cupcakes countless times, including for my sister's wedding. They are easy to mix up and make the perfect canvas for any flavor of buttercream frosting. *Nut-free*

PREP TIME: **10 minutes**

COOK TIME: **22 minutes**

1½ cups all-purpose flour

1½ teaspoons baking powder

¼ teaspoon salt

8 tablespoons (1 stick) unsalted butter, melted and slightly cooled

1 cup granulated sugar

2 large eggs, room temperature

1 large egg white, room temperature

½ cup milk, room temperature

1 tablespoon vanilla extract

1. Preheat the oven. Preheat the oven to 350°F. Line a cupcake pan with paper liners.

2. Combine the dry ingredients. In a small bowl, combine the flour, baking powder, and salt.

3. Combine the wet ingredients. In a large bowl, whisk together the butter and sugar. Mix in the eggs and egg white until incorporated. Stir in the milk and vanilla.

4. Add the dry ingredients. Add the dry ingredients to the wet ingredients, mixing until just combined.

5. Bake. Fill each cupcake cup about two-thirds full. Bake for 18 to 22 minutes, or until a toothpick inserted into the center comes out clean. Cool in the pan for 5 minutes, then remove the cupcakes and place them on a wire rack to cool completely. Frost the cooled cupcakes as desired.

SUBSTITUTION TIP: For a colorful and festive version of this cupcake, stir ⅓ cup of sprinkles into the batter.

Chocolate Cupcakes

Makes 15 cupcakes

Every baker needs a great chocolate cupcake recipe in their arsenal for special occasions. These cupcakes are perfect with Vanilla or Chocolate Buttercream (page 176). *Nut-free*

PREP TIME: **10 minutes**
COOK TIME: **14 minutes**

- ¾ cup all-purpose flour
- ½ cup unsweetened cocoa powder
- 1¼ teaspoons baking powder
- ½ teaspoon baking soda
- ½ teaspoon salt
- 2 large eggs, room temperature
- ¾ cup granulated sugar
- 1½ teaspoons vanilla extract
- ½ cup vegetable oil
- ½ cup sour cream

1. **Preheat the oven.** Preheat the oven to 350°F. Line two cupcake pans with paper liners.

2. **Combine the dry ingredients.** In a small bowl, combine the flour, cocoa powder, baking powder, baking soda, and salt.

3. **Combine the wet ingredients.** In a large bowl, whisk together the eggs, sugar, vanilla, oil, and sour cream.

4. **Add the dry ingredients.** Add the dry ingredients to the wet ingredients, mixing until just combined.

5. **Bake.** Fill each cupcake cup about two-thirds full. Bake for 12 to 14 minutes, or until a toothpick inserted into the center comes out clean. Cool in the pan for 5 minutes, then remove the cupcakes and place them on a cooling rack to cool completely. Frost the cooled cupcakes as desired.

SUBSTITUTION TIP: If you don't have sour cream, you can use buttermilk or Greek yogurt instead.

Lemon Cupcakes

Makes 12 cupcakes

These fluffy cupcakes are bright and bursting with lemon flavor. They are perfect frosted with Cream Cheese Frosting (page 175). Or, for an even richer lemon flavor, use Vanilla Buttercream (page 176) with 3 tablespoons of freshly squeezed lemon juice stirred in. *Nut-free*

PREP TIME: 10 minutes

COOK TIME: 20 minutes

1¼ cups cake flour

1½ teaspoons baking powder

¼ teaspoon salt

6 tablespoons (¾ stick) unsalted butter, room temperature

¾ cup granulated sugar

1 large egg, room temperature

1 large egg white, room temperature

1 teaspoon vanilla extract

⅓ cup freshly squeezed lemon juice

1½ tablespoons grated lemon zest

½ cup milk

1. **Preheat the oven.** Preheat the oven to 350°F. Line a cupcake pan with paper liners.

2. **Combine the dry ingredients.** In a small bowl, whisk together the flour, baking powder, and salt.

3. **Cream the butter and sugar.** In a large bowl, using an electric mixer, cream the butter and sugar until light and fluffy, about 2 minutes.

4. **Add the remaining wet ingredients.** Add the egg and egg white, one at a time, mixing well after each addition, and then beat in the vanilla, lemon juice, and lemon zest.

5. **Alternately add the dry ingredients and the milk.** Add the dry ingredients and the milk to the butter mixture in alternating batches, beginning and ending with the dry ingredients. Mix after each addition until just combined. Scrape down the bowl as needed. After the last addition of flour, increase the mixer speed to medium-high. Mix just until no traces of flour remain, about 30 seconds. Do not overbeat.

6. **Bake.** Fill each cupcake cup about two-thirds full. Bake for 18 to 20 minutes, or until a toothpick inserted into the center comes out clean. Cool in the pan for 5 minutes, then remove the cupcakes and place them on a cooling rack to cool completely. Frost the cooled cupcakes as desired.

SUBSTITUTION TIP: Make these into lemon-blueberry cupcakes by stirring in ¾ cup of fresh or frozen blueberries.

Banana Cupcakes

Makes 16 cupcakes

If you like banana bread, you're going to love these light,
fluffy cinnamon-spiced cupcakes. *Nut-free*

PREP TIME: 10 minutes

COOK TIME: 20 minutes

1½ cups all-purpose flour

1½ teaspoons baking powder

½ teaspoon baking soda

¼ teaspoon salt

1 tablespoon ground cinnamon

1 cup granulated sugar

8 tablespoons (1 stick) unsalted butter, melted and slightly cooled

2 large eggs, room temperature

1 teaspoon vanilla extract

½ cup sour cream

½ cup mashed ripe bananas (2 to 3 medium bananas)

1. Preheat the oven. Preheat the oven to 350°F. Line two cupcake pans with paper liners.

2. Combine the dry ingredients. In a small bowl, combine the flour, baking powder, baking soda, salt, and cinnamon.

3. Combine the wet ingredients. In a large bowl, whisk together the sugar, butter, eggs, vanilla, sour cream, and bananas.

4. Add the dry ingredients. Add the dry ingredients to the wet ingredients, mixing until just combined.

5. Bake. Fill each cupcake cup about two-thirds full. Bake for 18 to 20 minutes, or until a toothpick inserted into the center comes out clean. Cool in the pan for 5 minutes, then remove the cupcakes and place them on a cooling rack to cool completely. Frost the cooled cupcakes as desired.

TOPPING TIP: I love frosting these with a peanut butter frosting, which can be made by stirring 1 cup of peanut butter into Vanilla Buttercream (page 176).

Peanut Butter Cupcakes

Makes 30 cupcakes

These cupcakes are especially fun when frosted with Seven-Minute Icing (page 180), which brings a marshmallowy twist reminiscent of a fluffernutter sandwich.

PREP TIME: 10 minutes
COOK TIME: 20 minutes

- 3 cups cake flour
- 1 tablespoon baking powder
- ½ teaspoon salt
- 1 cup (2 sticks) unsalted butter, room temperature
- 2 cups granulated sugar
- 5 large eggs, room temperature
- 2 tablespoons vanilla extract
- ½ cup smooth peanut butter
- 1¼ cups buttermilk

1. **Preheat the oven.** Preheat the oven to 350°F. Line three cupcake pans with paper liners (or cook in batches).

2. **Combine the dry ingredients.** In a large bowl, whisk together the flour, baking powder, and salt.

3. **Cream the butter and sugar.** In a separate large bowl, using an electric mixer, cream the butter and sugar until light and fluffy, about 2 minutes.

4. **Add the remaining wet ingredients.** Add the eggs, one at a time, mixing well after each addition, and then beat in the vanilla and peanut butter.

5. **Alternately add the dry ingredients and the buttermilk.** Add the dry ingredients and the buttermilk to the butter mixture in alternating batches, beginning and ending with the dry ingredients. Mix after each addition until just combined. Scrape down the bowl as needed. After the last addition of flour, increase the mixer speed to medium-high. Beat just until no traces of flour remain, about 30 seconds. Do not overbeat.

6. **Bake.** Fill each cupcake cup about two-thirds full. Bake for 18 to 20 minutes, or until a toothpick inserted into the center comes out clean. Cool in the pan for 5 minutes, then remove the cupcakes and place them on a cooling rack to cool completely. Frost the cooled cupcakes as desired.

Maple-Bacon Cupcakes

Makes 18 cupcakes

These tender and moist cupcakes—made with brown sugar, maple syrup, and bacon—are the ultimate sweet and salty dessert or breakfast treat! *Nut-free*

PREP TIME: **15 minutes**

COOK TIME: **22 minutes**

2½ cups all-purpose flour

2 teaspoons baking powder

1 teaspoon baking soda

½ teaspoon salt

¾ teaspoon ground cinnamon

8 tablespoons (1 stick) unsalted butter, room temperature

½ cup light brown sugar

2 large eggs, room temperature

2 teaspoons vanilla extract

⅔ cup maple syrup

½ cup buttermilk

¾ cup crumbled cooked bacon, divided

1. **Preheat the oven.** Preheat the oven to 350°F. Line two cupcake pans with paper liners.

2. **Combine the dry ingredients.** In a medium bowl, whisk together the flour, baking powder, baking soda, salt, and cinnamon.

3. **Cream the butter and sugar.** In a large bowl, using an electric mixer, cream the butter and sugar until light and fluffy, about 2 minutes.

4. **Add the remaining wet ingredients.** Add the eggs, one at a time, mixing well after each addition. Mix in the vanilla and maple syrup.

5. **Alternately add the dry ingredients and the buttermilk.** Add the dry ingredients and the buttermilk to the butter mixture in alternating batches, beginning and ending with the dry ingredients. Mix after each addition until just combined. Using a rubber spatula, stir in ½ cup of bacon.

6. **Bake.** Fill each cupcake cup about two-thirds full. Bake for 18 to 22 minutes, or until a toothpick inserted into the center comes out clean. Cool in the pan for 5 minutes, then remove the cupcakes and place them on a cooling rack to cool completely. Frost the cooled cupcakes with your desired frosting and top each one with a sprinkle of the remaining ¼ cup of bacon.

TOPPING TIP: Make a maple buttercream frosting by stirring 1 teaspoon of maple extract or 3 tablespoons of maple syrup into Vanilla Buttercream (page 176).

Snickerdoodle Cupcakes

Makes 24 cupcakes

If you love snickerdoodle cookies, you'll swoon over these cupcakes. *Nut-free*

PREP TIME: 15 minutes
COOK TIME: 22 minutes

2½ cups all-purpose flour

2½ teaspoons baking powder

½ teaspoon baking soda

¼ teaspoon salt

2 teaspoons ground cinnamon

12 tablespoons (1½ sticks) unsalted butter, room temperature

½ cup granulated sugar

1 cup light brown sugar

2 large eggs, room temperature

2 teaspoons vanilla extract

1¼ cups buttermilk

1 tablespoon granulated sugar, for topping

1 teaspoon ground cinnamon, for topping

1. Preheat the oven. Preheat the oven to 375°F. Line two cupcake pans with paper liners.

2. Combine the dry ingredients. In a medium bowl, whisk together the flour, baking powder, baking soda, salt, and cinnamon.

3. Cream the butter and sugars. In a large bowl, using an electric mixer, cream the butter, granulated sugar, and brown sugar until light and fluffy, about 2 minutes.

4. Add the remaining wet ingredients. Add the eggs, one at a time, mixing well after each addition. Mix in the vanilla.

5. Alternately add the dry ingredients and the buttermilk. Add the dry ingredients and the buttermilk to the butter mixture in alternating batches, beginning and ending with the dry ingredients. Mix after each addition until just combined.

6. Make the topping. In a small bowl, combine the sugar and cinnamon for the topping. Sprinkle the topping over each cupcake before baking.

7. Bake. Fill each cupcake cup about two-thirds full. Bake for 18 to 22 minutes, or until a toothpick inserted into the center comes out clean. Cool in the pan for 5 minutes, then remove the cupcakes and place them on a cooling rack to cool completely. Frost the cooled cupcakes as desired.

TOPPING TIP: These are heavenly frosted with a cinnamon cream cheese frosting. Just add 1 tablespoon of cinnamon to Cream Cheese Frosting (page 175).

Gingerbread Cake

Makes 1 (9-inch) cake

Full of spices, molasses, and sweet honey, this gingerbread
cake is the perfect easy holiday-season dessert. Try it topped
with Stabilized Whipped Cream (page 179). *Nut-free*

PREP TIME: 15 minutes
COOK TIME: 35 minutes

2½ cups all-purpose flour

1½ teaspoons baking
soda

2 teaspoons ground
cinnamon

2 teaspoons ground
ginger

1 teaspoon ground cloves

½ teaspoon salt

½ cup dark brown sugar

½ cup vegetable oil

½ cup applesauce

1 large egg, room
temperature

½ cup molasses

½ cup honey

1 cup boiling water

1. Preheat the oven. Preheat the oven to 350°F. Lightly
coat a 9-inch round cake pan with cooking spray.

2. Combine the dry ingredients. In a medium bowl,
combine the flour, baking soda, cinnamon, ginger,
cloves, and salt.

3. Combine the wet ingredients. In a large bowl,
whisk together the sugar, oil, applesauce, egg, molasses,
and honey.

4. Add the dry ingredients. Add the dry ingredients to
the wet ingredients, mixing until just combined. Stir in
the boiling water.

5. Bake. Spread the batter in the pan in an even layer.
Bake for 30 to 35 minutes, or until a toothpick inserted
into the center comes out clean. Set the pan on a wire
rack and cool completely.

SUBSTITUTION TIP: If you don't have dark brown sugar,
substitute light brown sugar and add an extra
½ tablespoon of molasses.

Cinnamon Roll Cake

Makes 1 (9-by-13-inch) cake

This easy homemade vanilla cake batter has a sweet cinnamon sugar topping swirled through it. If you can't resist a big gooey cinnamon roll, then you are going to love this cake. *Nut-free*

PREP TIME: **15 minutes**
COOK TIME: **50 minutes**

FOR THE TOPPING

1 tablespoon ground cinnamon

1 cup light brown sugar

¼ teaspoon salt

FOR THE CAKE

3 cups all-purpose flour

2 teaspoons baking powder

½ teaspoon salt

1 cup granulated sugar

1 cup light brown sugar

1 cup (2 sticks) unsalted butter, melted and slightly cooled

4 large eggs, room temperature

2 teaspoons vanilla extract

1 cup milk

TO MAKE THE TOPPING

Make topping. In a small bowl, combine all the topping ingredients.

TO MAKE THE CAKE

1. Preheat the oven. Preheat the oven to 350°F. Lightly coat a 9-by-13-inch baking pan with cooking spray.

2. Combine the dry ingredients. In a medium bowl, combine the flour, baking powder, and salt.

3. Combine the wet ingredients. In a large bowl, whisk together the granulated sugar, brown sugar, butter, eggs, vanilla, and milk.

4. Add the dry ingredients. Add the dry ingredients to the wet ingredients, mixing until just combined.

5. Bake. Spread the batter in the pan in an even layer. Sprinkle the topping over the batter and swirl with a knife. Bake for 45 to 50 minutes until a toothpick inserted into the center comes out clean. Set the pan on a wire rack and cool completely. Frost the cooled cake as desired.

TOPPING TIP: I like to frost this cake with Powdered Sugar Glaze (page 170) or Cream Cheese Frosting (page 175).

Carrot Sheet Cake

Makes 1 (9-by-13-inch) cake

This perfectly spiced carrot sheet cake is easy to make, since the whole thing can be made in one bowl. I recommend grating the carrots by hand for the best texture and topping this cake with classic Cream Cheese Frosting (page 175). *Nut-free*

PREP TIME: 15 minutes
COOK TIME: 40 minutes

2 cups granulated sugar

½ cup vegetable oil

½ cup applesauce

4 large eggs, room temperature

2 cups all-purpose flour

½ teaspoon salt

1 teaspoon baking soda

1 teaspoon baking powder

2 teaspoons ground cinnamon

½ teaspoon ground nutmeg

½ teaspoon ground ginger

3 cups grated carrots (about 6 medium carrots)

1. Preheat the oven. Preheat the oven to 350°F. Lightly coat a 9-by-13-inch baking pan with cooking spray.

2. Combine the wet ingredients. In a large bowl, mix together the sugar, oil, applesauce, and eggs.

3. Add the dry ingredients. Add the flour, salt, baking soda, baking powder, cinnamon, nutmeg, and ginger. Stir to combine. Fold in the carrots.

4. Bake. Pour the batter into the pan. Bake for 35 to 40 minutes or until a toothpick inserted into the center comes out clean. Set the pan on a wire rack and cool completely. Frost the cooled cake as desired.

SUBSTITUTION TIP: For added crunch, fold in 1 cup of chopped, toasted pecans with the carrots in step 3.

Pumpkin Cake

Makes 1 (9-by-13-inch) cake

A moist spiced pumpkin cake that doesn't require an electric mixer and is ready to go in the oven in minutes? Sign me up! Finish this cake with a smooth layer of Cream Cheese Frosting (page 175). *Nut-free*

PREP TIME: **20 minutes**
COOK TIME: **35 minutes**

- 3 cups all-purpose flour
- ½ teaspoon salt
- 2 teaspoons baking soda
- 2 teaspoons ground cinnamon
- ¼ teaspoon ground nutmeg
- ¼ teaspoon ground cloves
- ½ teaspoon ground ginger
- 1 cup granulated sugar
- 1½ cups light brown sugar
- 1 cup vegetable oil
- 3 large eggs, room temperature
- 2 teaspoons vanilla extract
- 1 (15-ounce) can pumpkin purée

1. Preheat the oven. Preheat the oven to 350°F. Lightly coat a 9-by-13-inch baking pan with cooking spray.

2. Combine the dry ingredients. In a large bowl, whisk together the flour, salt, baking soda, cinnamon, nutmeg, cloves, and ginger.

3. Combine the wet ingredients. In a separate large bowl, whisk together the granulated sugar, brown sugar, oil, eggs, vanilla, and pumpkin purée until smooth and combined.

4. Add the dry ingredients. Add the dry ingredients to the wet ingredients, mixing until just combined.

5. Bake. Spread the batter in the pan in an even layer. Bake for 30 to 35 minutes, or until a toothpick inserted into the center comes out clean. Set the pan on a wire rack and cool completely. Frost the cooled cake as desired.

SUBSTITUTION TIP: If you're short on the individual spices, replace them with 1 tablespoon of pumpkin pie spice.

Orange Pound Cake

Makes 1 (10-inch) Bundt cake

When I first fell in love with baking, I enrolled in a class at a nearby culinary school. This bright, citrusy pound cake was one of the first recipes we learned to make. *Nut-free*

PREP TIME: 20 minutes
COOK TIME: 50 minutes

1 cup sour cream

1 teaspoon vanilla extract

2 tablespoons grated orange zest

2½ cups all-purpose flour

½ teaspoon baking powder

½ teaspoon baking soda

½ teaspoon salt

1 cup (2 sticks) unsalted butter, room temperature

2¼ cups granulated sugar

4 large eggs, room temperature

1. Preheat the oven. Preheat the oven to 350°F. Butter and flour a Bundt pan or two 9-by-5-inch loaf pans.

2. Combine the wet ingredients. In a small bowl, mix together the sour cream, vanilla, and orange zest.

3. Sift the dry ingredients. In a medium bowl, sift together the flour, baking powder, baking soda, and salt.

4. Cream the butter and sugar. In a large bowl, using an electric mixer, cream the butter and sugar until pale and fluffy, about 2 minutes.

5. Add the eggs. Add the eggs, one at a time, mixing well after each addition. Scrape down the bowl after each addition.

6. Alternately add the dry ingredients and the sour cream mixture. Add the dry ingredients and the sour cream mixture to the creamed butter and eggs in alternating batches, beginning and ending with the dry ingredients. Mix after each addition until just combined.

7. Bake. Spread the batter in the pan in an even layer. Bake for 50 minutes, or until a toothpick inserted into the center comes out clean. Cool in the pan for 10 minutes, then turn the cake out onto a wire rack and cool completely.

PREPARATION TIP: Make an orange glaze by adding 2 to 3 tablespoons of orange juice to Powdered Sugar Glaze (page 170). Pour the glaze over the top of the cake.

Chocolate Pudding Cake

Makes 1 (8-by-8-inch) cake

This quick, easy chocolate pudding cake forms a hot fudge layer underneath the cake as it bakes. Spoon some vanilla ice cream over it for an amazing sundae-style treat. *Nut-free*

PREP TIME: 10 minutes

COOK TIME: 25 minutes, plus 15 minutes to cool

FOR THE TOPPING

¼ cup light brown sugar

¼ cup granulated sugar

¼ cup unsweetened cocoa powder

1½ cups boiling water

FOR THE CAKE

1 cup all-purpose flour

1 cup granulated sugar

¼ cup unsweetened cocoa powder

2 teaspoons baking powder

½ teaspoon salt

½ cup milk

2 tablespoons vegetable oil

2 tablespoons butter

1½ teaspoons vanilla extract

TO MAKE THE TOPPING

Make the topping. In a small mixing bowl, combine the brown sugar, granulated sugar, and cocoa powder. Set aside.

TO MAKE THE CAKE

1. Preheat the oven. Preheat the oven to 350°F. Butter an 8-by-8-inch baking pan or coat it lightly with cooking spray.

2. Combine the dry ingredients. In a small bowl, combine the flour, sugar, cocoa powder, baking powder, and salt.

3. Combine the wet ingredients. In a large bowl, whisk together the milk, oil, butter, and vanilla.

4. Add the dry ingredients. Add the dry ingredients to the wet ingredients and mix until just combined.

5. Bake. Spread the batter in the pan in an even layer. Sprinkle the topping over the batter. Pour the boiling water over the topping. Do not stir. Bake for about 25 minutes, or until the top is set. Cool in the pan for about 15 minutes. Serve the cake warm, spooning it into bowls and drizzling a generous amount of the sauce over the cake.

SUBSTITUTION TIP: If you love dark chocolate, substitute dark cocoa powder for the regular unsweetened cocoa powder. It will yield a richer, darker, and more bittersweet chocolate cake.

Chocolate Zucchini Cake

Makes 1 (9-by-13-inch) cake

In the summertime, I always seem to have way too much zucchini on my hands. This wonderful, fudgy cake is great way to use it up. Try it with Chocolate Buttercream (page 176). *Nut-free*

PREP TIME: 15 minutes
COOK TIME: 1 hour

2 cups all-purpose flour

2¼ cups granulated sugar

¾ cup unsweetened cocoa powder

2 teaspoons baking soda

1 teaspoon baking powder

½ teaspoon salt

1 teaspoon vanilla extract

4 large eggs, room temperature

1 cup vegetable oil

3 cups grated zucchini

¾ cup semisweet chocolate chips

1. Preheat the oven. Preheat the oven to 350°F. Lightly coat a 9-by-13-inch baking pan with cooking spray.

2. Combine the dry ingredients. In a medium bowl, combine the flour, sugar, cocoa powder, baking soda, baking powder, and salt.

3. Combine the wet ingredients. In a large bowl, whisk together the vanilla, eggs, and oil until combined.

4. Add the dry ingredients. Add the dry ingredients to the wet ingredients and mix until just combined. Stir in the zucchini and chocolate chips.

5. Bake. Spread the batter in the pan in an even layer. Bake for 50 minutes to 1 hour, or until a toothpick inserted into the center comes out clean. Set the pan on a wire rack and cool completely. Frost the cooled cake as desired.

TROUBLESHOOTING TIP: The key to this moist cake is to not wring out the zucchini, ensuring it retains its moisture.

Summer Peach Crumb Cake

Makes 1 (9-inch) cake

This simple, fresh peach cake is the perfect summery treat!
Easy to make and topped with juicy ripe peaches, this cake
will quickly become a summertime favorite. *Nut-free*

PREP TIME: **20 minutes**

COOK TIME: **1 hour 10 minutes**

FOR THE TOPPING

1½ cups all-purpose flour

2 teaspoons ground cinnamon

12 tablespoons (1½ sticks) unsalted butter, melted

½ cup light brown sugar

½ teaspoon salt

FOR THE CAKE

1½ cups all-purpose flour

1½ teaspoons baking powder

½ teaspoon salt

6 tablespoons (¾ stick) unsalted butter, room temperature

1 cup granulated sugar

1 large egg, room temperature

½ cup milk

1 teaspoon vanilla extract

1 pound peaches, peeled and sliced (2 to 3 peaches)

TO MAKE THE TOPPING

Make the topping. In a small bowl, mix together all the topping ingredients until crumbly.

TO MAKE THE CAKE

1. Preheat the oven. Preheat the oven to 350°F. Lightly coat a 9-inch round cake pan with cooking spray.

2. Combine the dry ingredients. In a small bowl, whisk together the flour, baking powder, and salt.

3. Cream the butter and sugar. In a large bowl, using an electric mixer, cream the butter and sugar until light and fluffy, about 2 minutes.

4. Add the remaining wet ingredients. Mix in the egg, milk, and vanilla until just combined.

5. Add the dry ingredients. Add the dry ingredients to the wet ingredients, mixing until just combined.

6. Bake. Spread the batter in the pan in an even layer. Top with the peaches. Sprinkle the topping over the batter in an even layer. Bake for 10 minutes, then reduce the oven temperature to 325°F and bake until golden brown and a toothpick inserted into the center comes out clean, 50 minutes to 1 hour. Set the pan on a wire rack and cool completely.

SUBSTITUTION TIP: Substitute another fresh fruit such as plums, cherries, or strawberries for the peaches.

Blueberry-Lemon Coffee Cake

Makes 1 (9-by-13-inch) cake

Bursting with blueberries, lemon zest, and Greek yogurt, this cake is crowned with a crunchy cinnamon crumble. *Nut-free*

PREP TIME: 20 minutes
COOK TIME: 1 hour

FOR THE TOPPING

1 cup light brown sugar

½ cup granulated sugar

1½ tablespoons ground cinnamon

½ teaspoon salt

1 cup (2 sticks) unsalted butter, melted and slightly cooled

2½ cups all-purpose flour

FOR THE CAKE

2½ cups all-purpose flour

1 teaspoon baking soda

¾ teaspoon baking powder

½ teaspoon salt

12 tablespoons (1½ sticks) unsalted butter, room temperature

1½ cups granulated sugar

2 large eggs, room temperature

1½ teaspoons vanilla extract

1¼ cups Greek yogurt

1 tablespoon grated lemon zest

2 cups blueberries (fresh or frozen)

TO MAKE THE TOPPING

Make the topping. In a small bowl, whisk together the brown sugar, granulated sugar, cinnamon, and salt. Stir in the melted butter. Add the flour and stir with a fork until moist clumps form.

TO MAKE THE CAKE

1. Preheat the oven. Preheat the oven to 350°F. Lightly coat a 9-by-13-inch baking pan with cooking spray.

2. Combine the dry ingredients. In a medium bowl, whisk together the flour, baking soda, baking powder, and salt.

3. Cream the butter and sugar. In a large bowl, using an electric mixer, cream the butter and sugar until light and fluffy, about 2 minutes.

4. Add the remaining wet ingredients. Add the eggs, one at a time, mixing well after each addition. Scrape down the bowl as needed. Stir in the vanilla, yogurt, and lemon zest.

5. Add the dry ingredients. Add one-third of the dry ingredients and mix until just incorporated. Repeat two times to use up all the flour. Fold in the blueberries.

6. Bake. Spread the batter in the pan in an even layer. Sprinkle the topping over the batter. Bake for 1 hour, or until a toothpick inserted into the center comes out clean and the topping is a deep golden brown and slightly crisp. Set the pan on a wire rack and let cool completely.

TOPPING TIP: Drizzle with Powdered Sugar Glaze (page 170).

Apple-Walnut Cake

Makes 1 (9-inch) cake

This moist snack cake spiced with cinnamon, sweet apples, and walnuts doesn't even need a frosting; simply dust with a touch of powdered sugar and amaze your guests.

PREP TIME: **20 minutes**
COOK TIME: **45 minutes**

- 8 tablespoons (1 stick) unsalted butter, room temperature
- ½ cup granulated sugar
- ½ cup light brown sugar
- 2 large eggs, room temperature
- 1 teaspoon vanilla extract
- 1¼ cups all-purpose flour
- 1 teaspoon baking soda
- 2 teaspoons ground cinnamon
- ½ teaspoon salt
- 1½ cups shredded apple
- ½ cup toasted chopped walnuts or pecans

1. Preheat the oven. Preheat the oven to 350°F. Butter and flour a 9-inch round cake pan.

2. Cream the butter and sugars. In large bowl, using an electric mixer, cream the butter, granulated sugar, and brown sugar until light and fluffy, about 2 minutes.

3. Add the remaining ingredients. Add the eggs, one at a time, mixing well after each addition. Stir in the vanilla, flour, baking soda, cinnamon, and salt. Stir in the apples and walnuts.

4. Bake. Spread the batter in the pan in an even layer. Bake for 40 to 45 minutes, or until a toothpick inserted into the center comes out clean. Cool in the pan for 10 minutes, then turn the cake out onto a wire rack and cool completely.

SUBSTITUTION TIP: For more spice and flavor, swap out the cinnamon and use apple pie spice instead.

Pineapple Upside-Down Cake

Makes 1 (9-inch) cake

Baking a cake upside down is a technique that dates to when baking was done in cast iron skillets. This modern version yields a buttery cake topped with mouthwatering caramelized pineapple. *Nut-free*

PREP TIME: **20 minutes**
COOK TIME: **50 minutes**

FOR THE TOPPING

- 1 (20-ounce) can pineapple slices
- 4 tablespoons (½ stick) unsalted butter, melted
- ⅔ cup light brown sugar
- 14 maraschino cherries

FOR THE CAKE

- 1½ cups all-purpose flour
- 1½ teaspoons baking powder
- ¼ teaspoon baking soda
- ¼ teaspoon salt
- ½ cup (1 stick) unsalted butter, room temperature
- 1 cup granulated sugar
- 2 large eggs, room temperature
- 2½ teaspoons vanilla extract
- ⅔ cup buttermilk

TO MAKE THE TOPPING

1. Preheat the oven. Preheat the oven to 350°F. Lightly coat a 9-inch round cake pan with cooking spray.

2. Make the topping. Drain the pineapple. In the 9-inch round pan, mix together the butter and sugar. Place the pineapple slices in the sugar mixture (8 on the bottom and cut the remaining 3 slices in half and place around the sides of the pan). Place a cherry in the center of each pineapple slice, in the center of the pan, and around the sides.

TO MAKE THE CAKE

1. Combine the dry ingredients. In a small bowl, combine the flour, baking powder, baking soda, and salt.

2. Cream the butter and sugar. In a large bowl, using an electric mixer, cream the butter and sugar until light and fluffy, about 2 minutes. Add the eggs, one at a time, mixing well after each addition. Mix in the vanilla.

3. Alternately add the dry ingredients and the buttermilk. Add the dry ingredients and the buttermilk to the creamed butter in alternating batches, beginning and ending with dry ingredients. Mix after each addition until just combined.

4. Bake. Bake for 45 to 50 minutes, or until a toothpick inserted into the center comes out clean. Cool in the pan for 5 minutes. Loosen the edges, place a serving platter over the pan, and invert the cake onto the platter.

Vanilla Layer Cake

Makes 1 (9-inch) cake

Every baker needs a great vanilla cake recipe in their arsenal. This is a great option, and a wonderful blank canvas for myriad fillings and frostings, including Vanilla or Chocolate Buttercream (page 176) or Berry Buttercream (page 178). *Nut-free*

PREP TIME: 20 minutes

COOK TIME: 35 minutes

3¼ cups cake flour

1 tablespoon baking powder

1 teaspoon salt

8 tablespoons (1 stick) unsalted butter, room temperature

½ cup vegetable oil

2 cups granulated sugar

4 large eggs, room temperature

1 tablespoon vanilla extract

1½ cups buttermilk

1. Preheat the oven. Preheat the oven to 350°F. Butter and flour two 9-inch round cake pans.

2. Combine the dry ingredients. In a large bowl, whisk together the flour, baking powder, and salt.

3. Cream the butter and sugar. In a separate large bowl, using an electric mixer, cream the butter, oil, and sugar until light and fluffy, about 2 minutes.

4. Add the eggs and vanilla. Add the eggs, one at a time, mixing well after each addition. Scrape down the bowl after each addition. Mix in the vanilla.

5. Alternately add the dry ingredients and the buttermilk. Add the dry ingredients and the buttermilk to the creamed butter in alternating batches, beginning and ending with the dry ingredients. Mix after each addition until just combined.

6. Bake. Pour half of the batter into each pan. Bake for 30 to 35 minutes, or until golden brown around the edges and a toothpick inserted into the center comes out clean. Cool in the pans for 5 minutes, then turn the cakes out onto a wire rack to cool completely. Frost the cooled cake first between the layers, then on the top, and then around the sides.

PREPARATION TIP: Try adding fruit curd, preserves, or even sliced strawberries between the layers.

Chocolate Layer Cake

Makes 1 (9-inch) cake

Perfect for every birthday table's centerpiece, this cake is light, made in just one bowl, and brimming with sweetness. Besting any boxed option, this one's for the kids (and the kids-at-heart). Go all in on the chocolate and frost this with Chocolate Buttercream (page 176). *Nut-free*

PREP TIME: 20 minutes
COOK TIME: 35 minutes

2¼ cups all-purpose flour

2 teaspoons baking soda

¾ cup unsweetened cocoa powder

½ teaspoon salt

½ cup vegetable oil

1 cup light brown sugar

1 cup granulated sugar

3 large eggs, room temperature

1½ teaspoons vanilla extract

1 cup buttermilk

1 cup boiling water

1. Preheat the oven. Preheat the oven to 350°F. Butter and flour two 9-inch round cake pans.

2. Combine the dry ingredients. In a large bowl, whisk together the flour, baking soda, cocoa powder, and salt.

3. Combine the wet ingredients. In a medium bowl, whisk together the oil, brown sugar, granulated sugar, eggs, vanilla, and buttermilk until smooth.

4. Combine the wet and dry ingredients. Pour the wet mixture into the flour mixture and whisk to combine. Stir in the boiling water.

5. Bake. Pour half of the batter into each pan. Bake for 30 to 35 minutes, or until a toothpick inserted into the center comes out clean. Cool in the pans for 5 minutes, then turn the cakes out onto a wire rack to cool completely. Frost the cooled cake first between the layers and then on the top and around the sides.

SUBSTITUTION TIP: For a mocha flavor, add 1 teaspoon of espresso powder to the boiling water.

Red Velvet Layer Cake

Makes 1 (9-inch) cake

This iconic showstopper has a slight buttermilk tang and a hint of chocolate, making this cake perfect for Valentine's Day, Christmas, or any festive occasion. *Nut-free*

PREP TIME: 20 minutes
COOK TIME: 35 minutes

2½ cups cake flour

1½ teaspoons baking soda

3 tablespoons unsweetened cocoa powder

1 teaspoon salt

½ cup vegetable oil

1½ cups granulated sugar

2 large eggs, room temperature

2 tablespoons red food coloring

1½ teaspoons vanilla extract

1 cup buttermilk

1 tablespoon distilled white vinegar

1. Preheat the oven. Preheat the oven to 350°F. Butter and flour two 9-inch round cake pans.

2. Combine the dry ingredients. In a large bowl, whisk together the flour, baking soda, cocoa powder, and salt.

3. Combine the wet ingredients. In a medium bowl, mix the oil, sugar, eggs, food coloring, vanilla, buttermilk, and vinegar until smooth.

4. Combine the wet and dry ingredients. Pour the wet mixture into flour mixture and, using a rubber spatula, stir to combine.

5. Bake. Pour half of the batter into each pan. Bake for 30 to 35 minutes, or until a toothpick inserted into the center comes out clean. Cool in the pans for 5 minutes, then turn the cakes out onto a wire rack to cool completely. Frost the cooled cake first between the layers and then on the top and around the sides.

PREPARATION TIP: A classic frosting pairing is, of course, Cream Cheese Frosting (page 175). Or try Fluffy White (Boiled Milk) Icing (page 174) for something a bit different.

Coconut Layer Cake

Makes 1 (9-inch) cake

Packed full of tender, sweet coconut, this moist cake is a coconut lover's dream. Coconut Buttercream (page 177) adds the perfect finishing touch. *Nut-free*

PREP TIME: 30 minutes

COOK TIME: 26 to 30 minutes

1 cup canned coconut milk

4 tablespoons (½ stick) unsalted butter, melted

⅓ cup vegetable oil

2 cups cake flour

2 teaspoons baking powder

1¼ teaspoons salt

4 large eggs, room temperature

2 cups granulated sugar

1 teaspoon vanilla extract

2 teaspoons coconut extract

1 cup shredded sweetened coconut

1. **Preheat the oven.** Preheat the oven to 325°F. Butter and flour two 9-inch cake pans.

2. **Combine the wet ingredients.** In a small bowl, mix together the coconut milk, butter, and oil.

3. **Sift the dry ingredients.** In a separate small bowl, sift together the flour, baking powder, and salt.

4. **Mix the eggs and sugar.** In a large bowl, using an electric mixer with a whisk attachment set on medium-high, beat the eggs, sugar, vanilla, and coconut extract until thickened and light gold in color, about 2 minutes. The batter should fall in thick ribbons from the whisk.

5. **Alternately add the dry ingredients and the coconut milk mixture.** Add the dry ingredients and the coconut milk mixture to the eggs and sugar in alternating batches, beginning and ending with the dry ingredients. Mix after each addition until just combined. Stir in the shredded coconut.

6. **Bake.** Pour half of the batter into each pan. Bake until a toothpick inserted into the center comes out clean and the top feels set, 26 to 30 minutes. Cool in the pans for 10 minutes, then turn the cakes out onto a wire rack and cool completely. Frost the cooled cake first between the layers and then on the top and around the sides.

SUBSTITUTION TIP: If you can't find canned coconut milk, replace it with whole milk.

Hummingbird Layer Cake

Makes 1 (9-inch) cake

This Southern favorite is chock-full of spices, bananas, pecans, and pineapple and is typically frosted with Cream Cheese Frosting (page 175).

PREP TIME: **20 minutes**
COOK TIME: **30 minutes**

3 cups all-purpose flour

1 cup granulated sugar

1 cup light brown sugar

1 teaspoon baking soda

1½ teaspoons ground cinnamon

½ teaspoon ground allspice

1 teaspoon salt

1½ cups vegetable oil

3 large eggs, room temperature

1 (8-ounce) can crushed pineapple, drained

2 cups mashed bananas (5 to 6 bananas)

1½ teaspoons vanilla extract

1 cup chopped pecans

1. Preheat the oven. Preheat the oven to 350°F. Butter and flour two 9-inch round cake pans.

2. Sift the dry ingredients. In a large bowl, sift together the flour, granulated sugar, brown sugar, baking soda, cinnamon, allspice, and salt.

3. Combine the wet ingredients. In a separate large bowl, combine the oil, eggs, pineapple, bananas, vanilla, and pecans.

4. Add the dry ingredients. Add the dry ingredients to the wet ingredients, mixing until just combined.

5. Bake. Pour half of the batter into each pan. Bake for 25 to 30 minutes, or until a toothpick inserted into the center comes out clean. Cool in the pans for 5 minutes, then loosen the edges and turn the cakes out onto a wire rack to cool completely. Frost the cooled cake first between the layers and then on the top and around the sides.

SUBSTITUTION TIP: You can substitute ¼ teaspoon of cinnamon, ¼ teaspoon of cloves, and a pinch of ground nutmeg for the allspice.

Lemon-Raspberry Layer Cake

Makes 1 (9-inch) cake

Sweet raspberries and tart lemon play wonderfully off each other in this light and fluffy cake, making it the perfect treat for a Mother's Day or Easter brunch. *Nut-free*

PREP TIME: 20 minutes
COOK TIME: 30 minutes

2¾ cups all-purpose flour

1⅔ cups granulated sugar

1 tablespoon baking powder

½ teaspoon baking soda

¾ teaspoon salt

12 tablespoons (1½ sticks) unsalted butter, room temperature

1 tablespoon grated lemon zest

4 large egg whites, room temperature

1 large egg, room temperature

1 cup milk

1½ teaspoons vanilla extract

⅓ cup freshly squeezed lemon juice

1½ cups fresh raspberries

1. Preheat the oven. Preheat the oven to 350°F. Butter and flour two 9-inch round cake pans.

2. Combine the dry ingredients and butter. In a large bowl, using an electric mixer set on low, mix together the flour, sugar, baking powder, baking soda, and salt. Add the butter and mix until crumbly. Add the lemon zest.

3. Add the eggs. Add the egg whites, one at a time, then the whole egg, beating well after each addition. Scrape down the bowl after each addition.

4. Add the remaining ingredients. In a small bowl, whisk together the milk, vanilla, and lemon juice. Add this mixture, one-third at a time, to the batter. Beat for 1 to 2 minutes after each addition, until fluffy. Scrape down the bowl as needed. Fold in the raspberries.

5. Bake. Pour half of the batter into each pan. Bake for 25 to 30 minutes, or until a toothpick inserted into the center comes out clean. Cool in the pans for 10 minutes, then turn the cakes out onto a wire rack to cool completely. Frost the cooled cake first between the layers and then on the top and around the sides.

SUBSTITUTION TIP: You can also use frozen raspberries. To mix up the fruity element, try blueberries instead of raspberries. To finish, try Cream Cheese Frosting (page 175) with 2 tablespoons of freshly squeezed lemon juice added in.

Jalapeño-Cheddar Biscuits **PAGE 151**

8

Beautiful Breads, Biscuits, and Crackers

Bottle Cap Locket

Need a thoughtful gift for your mom or grandma? This bottle cap locket is a great way to show your love!

What You Need:

- ✓ 2 bottle caps
- ✓ 3-inch piece of ribbon
- ✓ Small photo
- ✓ Scrapbook paper
- ✓ Marker
- ✓ White craft glue
- ✓ Yarn or cord

1 Glue one end of the ribbon inside one of the bottle caps.

2 Glue the other end of the ribbon inside the second bottle cap, leaving about an inch of ribbon between the two bottle caps.

3 Cut your photo to fit inside the bottom bottle cap and glue it in place.

4 Cut out a piece of scrapbook paper and draw or write a message on it. Glue it inside the other bottle cap.

5 Place the yarn or cord onto the center of the ribbon and glue in place.

6 Close the locket by placing the two bottle caps together.

TOP TIP: If you want, you can put two photos in your locket—how about one of you and one of Mom?

Button Hair Flair

Grab a handful of buttons and give your hair accessories a whole new look. You'll look cute as a button!

1 Use hot glue to attach buttons to your hair accessories.

2 Layer the buttons for a fun, 3-D look.

Button Necklace

Who knew that something so easy could be so great? This is a fab project for sleepovers, camp, or just hanging out with friends. Make one to match your favorite outfit, or in your school colors. Try using big or small buttons, or working in a pattern.

1 Decide what buttons you would like on your necklace.

2 Thread the cord through one hole in a button.

3 Repeat step 2 until you have as many buttons as you want.

4 Tie the necklace around your neck.

ON THE BUTTON

The word button comes from the French *bouton* and means bud or round object.

stuff to play

Bottle Cap Spinning Top

You might think this is over the top, but we think it'll make your head spin! Here's how you can make your very own top with a recycled plastic bottle cap and a toothpick.

1 Find the center of the plastic bottle cap and carefully push the pushpin through it. Many plastic caps have a dot in the center, so aim for that. If your hole is off-center your top could turn off-balance.

2 Poke the end of the toothpick into the hole through the bottom and, using a twisting motion, carefully work the toothpick through. You want about one third of the toothpick to show through the top of the cap.

3 If you would like to decorate your top, you can add beads to the toothpick, securing them with glue, or wrap a little decorative tape around it.

4 Add a dab of glue to hold the toothpick in place.

5 To play, hold the top so that the toothpick is touching the table and spin the long end of the toothpick with your fingers.

CD Spinner

Here's another great way to make a top with a bottle cap and a few other recyclables. You will love how easy this one is to put in motion! A quick flick of the wrist and you'll be twirling and spinning all afternoon.

What You Need:
- ✓ Recycled CD/DVD
- ✓ Duct tape or patterned scrapbook paper
- ✓ Plastic bottle cap
- ✓ Practice golf ball
- ✓ White craft glue
- ✓ Craft knife or scissors

1 Cover the printed side of the CD with duct tape.

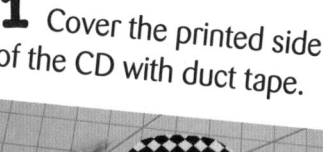
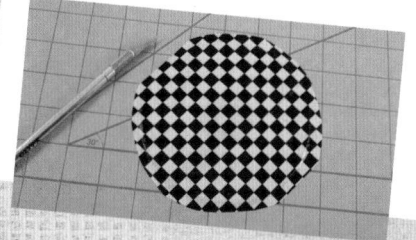

2 Trim around the edges with a craft knife or scissors and stick the excess tape around to the back of the CD.

3 If using scrapbook paper, glue the paper to the CD, then trim the edges around the CD.

4 Glue the plastic lid to the top of the CD at the center.

5 Glue the golf ball to the back of the CD at the center.

6 Let the glue dry completely.

7 To play, hold the plastic lid handle with the golf ball touching the surface you are spinning on. Give the CD a quick spin!

TOP TIP: Practice golf balls are much lighter than regulation golf balls. They are similar to a Wiffle ball and can be found in the sporting goods department of any discount department store.

Clothespin Car

We're really going to get your wheels turning with this one…literally! These little cars are great fun to push across the floor or down a homemade ramp. You can even decorate them using paint or markers.

1 Insert one of the twist ties into a hole in one of the buttons.

2 Thread about an inch or so of the twist tie back through a second hole.

3 Twist the tie tightly at the back of the button.

4 Thread one of the straw pieces onto the twist tie.

5 Thread the open end of the twist tie through the second button, then thread it back through the second hole and twist together like you did in step 3.

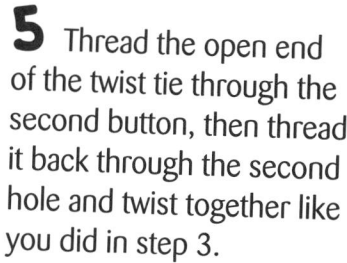

6 Repeat steps 1-5 for the second pair of buttons.

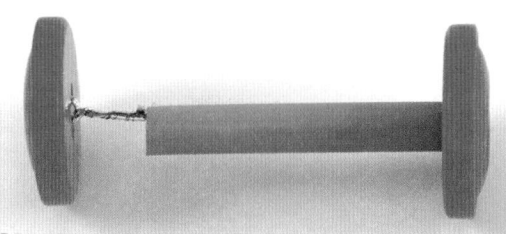

7 Open the clothespin and place the straw from one set of wheels in the hole of the clothespin opening. Close the clothespin. The straw will flatten a bit, but the twist tie should be able to turn freely inside the straw.

8 Add a dab of white glue to the back of the clothespin near the spring.

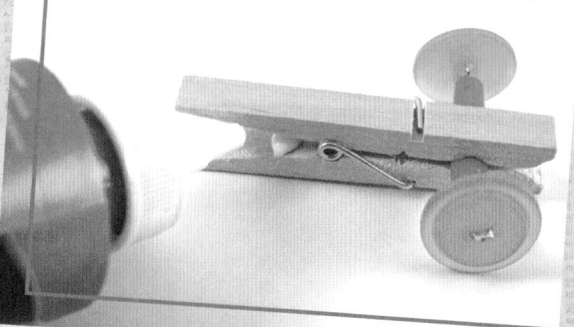

9 Insert the second set of wheels onto the glue. Allow the glue to dry.

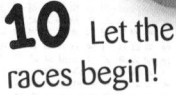

10 Let the races begin!

ON THE BUTTON

The oldest button ever found was in the Indus Valley Civilization, in what is now Pakistan. The button is made of a curved shell and dates back 5,000 years!

23

What You Need:
- ✓ Craft stick
- ✓ Scissors
- ✓ Plastic lid
- ✓ Hot glue gun
- ✓ Scrapbook paper

Sailboat

This project is really going to float your boat! Dig into your recycling bin and get ready for an afternoon of sailboat races.

1 Cut the craft stick in half.

2 Attach the cut side of the craft stick to the underside of the plastic lid using hot glue, so it is standing straight up.

3 Cut a strip of scrapbook paper and fold in half to create a flag. Glue the flag around the top of the craft stick.

4 Place your sailboat in the water and sail away!

Tiddlywinks

Have you ever played tiddlywinks? It's a game that became popular in the late 1800s. Players compete to see who can score the most points flipping disks (or "winks") into a pot or bucket. No need to buy a set; you can play with buttons! Make multiple buckets for you and your friends to practice with before the game begins.

1 Cut card stock into 8½" x 2" strips.

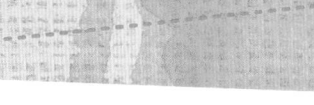

2 Coil card stock strips into cups and secure with tape.

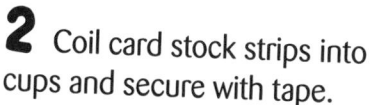

3 To practice, press the large button onto the edge of a small button. Press down and at the same time drag the large button off the small button. The small button will jump into the air.

4 When you are ready to play, take turns attempting to flip a button into a bucket. If your button goes in the bucket, you score a point and get another turn. First player to score 10 points wins!

TOP TIP: It helps to play on a large piece of felt—keeps the buttons from slipping!

Checkers

What You Need:

- ✓ White card stock
- ✓ Colored pencil
- ✓ Ruler
- ✓ 12 buttons of one color
- ✓ 12 buttons of a second color

Playing checkers is lots of fun, but if you don't have a game board that doesn't mean you're out of luck. You can easily make your own checkerboard and use buttons as the checkers!

1 Cut card stock into an 8" x 8" square.

2 Measure and mark the card stock in 1-inch increments all the way around the four sides of the paper.

3 Use a ruler to create a grid of eight squares across and eight squares down.

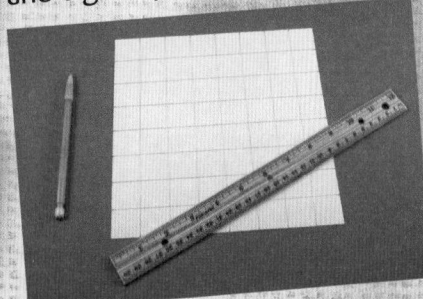

4 Color in every other square to create a checkerboard pattern.

5 Use buttons as playing pieces, each player using a different color.

26

Outdoor Tic Tac Toe

Here's a fun and really simple way to pass the time during the lazy days of summer...a game of outdoor tic tac toe! We used a piece of chalk, but you can even draw your tic tac toe board with a rock.

1 Draw a tic tac toe game board with chalk on the sidewalk. If you don't have chalk, scratch the pavement with a rock to draw the board.

2 One player uses buttons as pieces and the other player uses bottle caps, in place of X's and O's.

3 Each player takes a turn placing a game piece on the board. The person who succeeds in lining up three of their pieces in a row, either diagonally, vertically, or horizontally, wins!

Button Button Game

Choose one player to be "it." The other players stand or sit in a circle with their hands in front of them, palms together. "It" takes the button and goes around the circle to each player and puts the button in one player's hands, but pretends to put the button in every player's hands. The idea is to not let anyone see who has the button.

"It" says, "Button, button, who's got the button?" and asks each player to make a guess. The first person to guess correctly wins and becomes "it" for the next round. Note: When it's the player with the button's turn to guess, he or she must guess someone else so no one will know who has it!

What You Need:

- ✓ Pliers
- ✓ 15 bottle caps
- ✓ Canning lid
- ✓ Strong bond glue (available at hardware stores or in the craft aisle)
- ✓ 12-inch wooden dowel

Bottle Cap Flower

Use up some of those extra bottle caps you've been saving to make some fun and funky flowers. Perfect for your garden, these are also great for dressing up a flowerpot!

1 Use a pair of pliers to bend 12 of the bottle caps in half, like a book. Set them aside.

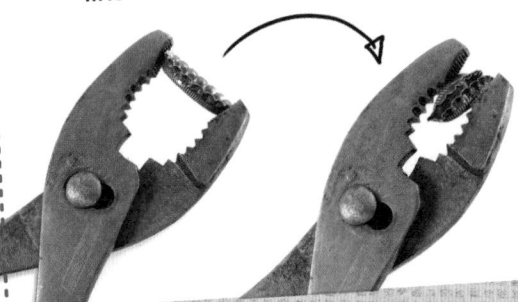

2 Glue a bottle cap to the center of the canning lid.

3 Glue the 12 bent bottle caps to the canning lid, going around the center bottle cap. Group them in sets of two, so that you create six flower petals.

5 Finally, glue the dowel to the back of the flower.

6 Allow the glue to dry completely and then find a great spot for your flower in your garden—or make a bunch for a bouquet!

4 Glue two bottle caps to the sides of the dowel as leaves.

TOP TIP: If you don't plan on "planting" your flowers outside, you can use hot glue for this project.

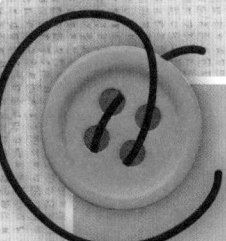

ON THE BUTTON

The earliest buttons were used for decoration rather than as fasteners. Buttons with buttonholes first appeared in the thirteenth century in Germany. By the fourteenth century, buttons were widespread throughout Europe.

What You Need:

- ✓ String
- ✓ Needle (with a hole big enough for your string)
- ✓ Plastic lid
- ✓ Peanut butter or sunflower seed butter
- ✓ Birdseed
- ✓ Cookie sheet

Bird Feeder

Have you ever made a pinecone bird feeder? This project uses the same idea, but you are recycling some plastic lids in the process! If you have a peanut allergy, try sunflower seed butter instead!

1 Cut a piece of string about 18 inches long.

2 Thread the needle and poke it through the top of the plastic lid.

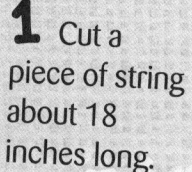

3 Tie the thread in a knot to secure it to the lid.

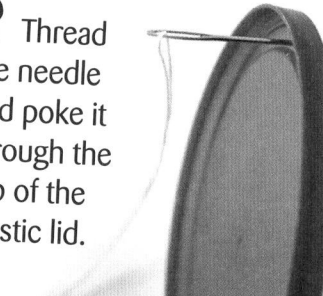

4 Fill the lid with peanut butter.

5 Spread birdseed out on the cookie sheet.

6 Place the lid, peanut butter side down, into the birdseed.

7 Lift it out of the birdseed and hang in a tree!

TOP TIP: Squirrels will love these treats so try to hang them where the squirrels can't reach. You should also hang them near a branch where the birds can perch.

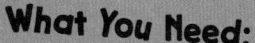

What You Need:

✓ Large plastic lid
   (margarine container
   or larger)

✓ Scissors

✓ Needle and string

Wind Spinner

Hang this simple wind spinner from a tree and watch it whirl and twirl. For this simple craft all you need is a large plastic lid, a pair of scissors, and some string!

1 Use the scissors to poke a small slit in the center of the plastic lid.

2 Starting at the slit, cut a coil from the center of the lid to the outer edge of the lid. Don't cut through the outer edge; leave it in a ring.

3 Thread the needle and poke it through the center of the coil.

4 Tie the string in a knot to secure it to the center of the coil.

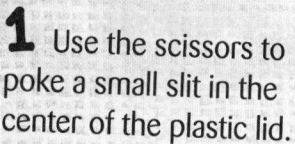

5 Hang it from a tree!

Rainbow Wind Chime

Create a beautiful rainbow of buttons, or if you prefer, mix up the colors or go bold with all one color! Doesn't matter which way you go— you'll still wow your friends with this awesome project.

What You Need:

- ✓ 12 metal canning lids
- ✓ Hammer and nail
- ✓ Outdoor craft paint (optional)
- ✓ 1 large, sturdy plastic lid
- ✓ Pushpin
- ✓ String
- ✓ Scissors
- ✓ 16 pony beads
- ✓ Hot glue gun
- ✓ Lots of buttons
- ✓ 12 tri-beads
- ✓ White craft glue

1 Use hammer and nail to poke a hole in the top of each canning lid.

2 If you'd like, paint each of the lids, front and back, and let them dry. Set aside.

3 Use a pushpin to poke four evenly spaced holes into the inside rim of the large plastic lid. This will be for your hanger.

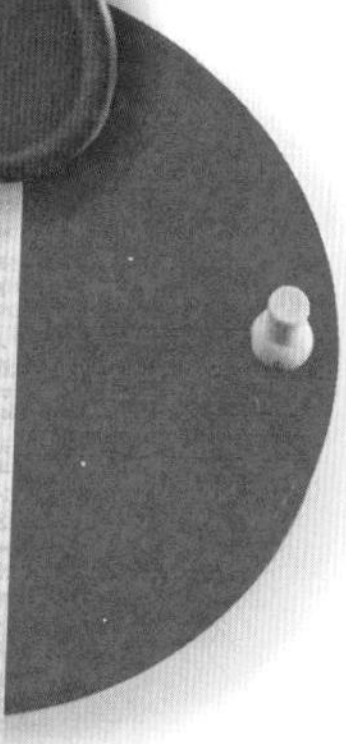

4 Use the pushpin to poke twelve evenly spaced holes on the top of the plastic lid.

5 Measure and cut 16 pieces of string, about 24 inches long. Tie a pony bead to the end of each string. Set four strings aside and thread the remaining 12 strings through the holes in the top of the lid so the pony beads hold them in place. Tack beads in place with a little hot glue.

6 Thread four large buttons through one string and add a tri-bead. Add some white glue between each button and the bead to hold them in place.

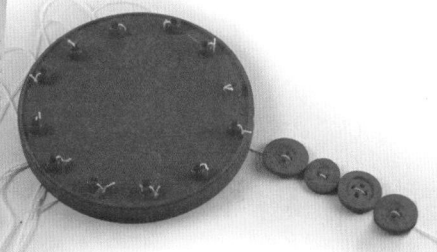

7 Repeat step 6 for each string, adding a few more buttons each time to create a tiered effect.

8 Tie a canning lid to the end of each string.

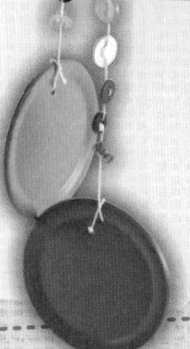

9 Use the four remaining strings to create the hanger. Thread each one through a hole in the side of the lid and secure with a knot. Gather all four strings together and tie in a knot.

TOP TIP: We made our wind chime to look like the colors of a rainbow, using all of the same color buttons and lid on one string. You can follow our colors, or make up a color scheme of your own!

What You Need:

- ✓ Jar lid
- ✓ Hammer and nail
- ✓ Jump rings
- ✓ String
- ✓ 4 pony beads
- ✓ Flat nosed pliers
- ✓ Bottle caps
- ✓ Hot glue gun
- ✓ Charms (optional)

Bottle Cap Wind Chime

We hope you've been saving all those bottle tops! Here's a great outdoor project you can make in an afternoon. Perfect for hanging on the porch or in the garden.

1 Use a hammer and nail to poke three holes in the rim of the jar lid. Space the holes evenly around the rim.

2 Turn the lid upside down and poke four holes in the flat top of the lid.

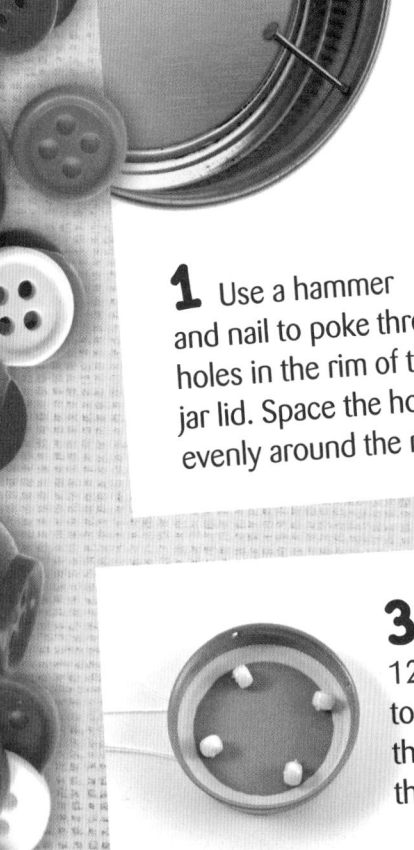

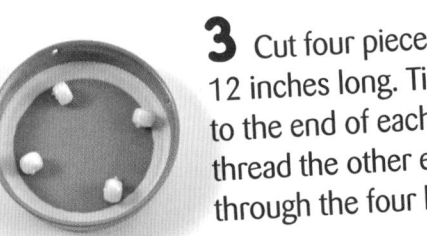

3 Cut four pieces of string, each 12 inches long. Tie a pony bead to the end of each string and thread the other end of each string through the four holes in the lid.

4 Turn the lid right side up, grasp all the strings, and tie them together.

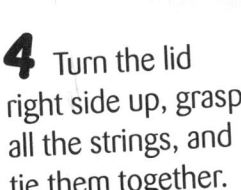

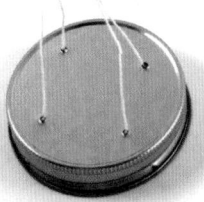

5 Use flat nose pliers to add three jump rings to each of the three holes on the rim.

6 Use the hammer and nail to poke two holes in each bottle cap (see page 9). Make the holes at the top and bottom, right where the cap begins to bend.

7 Add a jump ring to the top hole of each bottle cap.

8 Add a jump ring to the bottom hole of each bottle cap.

9 Connect the bottle caps together by using an additional jump ring between each cap. Make three chains as long as you like (we used seven for each chain).

10 Finish each chain of caps by attaching a charm to the end, if you like.

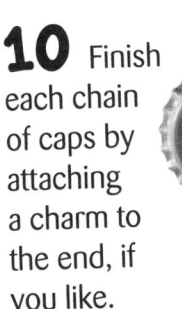

11 Attach the chains to the jump rings on the lid and hang from a tree or porch.

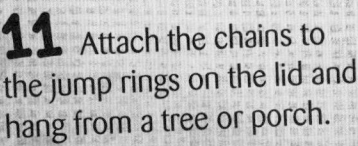

- ✓ Plaster of paris
- ✓ Measuring cup
- ✓ Bowl
- ✓ Water
- ✓ Large spoon for mixing
- ✓ Disposable aluminum pie plate
- ✓ Buttons
- ✓ Paintbrush
- ✓ Gloss sealer

Garden Stone

Next time you tag along with Mom or Dad to the hardware store, ask them to grab a container of plaster of paris for you. It's super easy to mix up, and with a handful or two of colorful buttons you'll quickly be on your way to creating beautiful garden art.

1 First you'll want to plan out your design. Plaster of paris dries pretty quickly, so you won't have time for planning once you pour the mixture into the pan! If you're making a picture like a flower or a butterfly, lay all your buttons out in front of you first.

2 Mix two cups of plaster of paris powder and one cup of water in a bowl. Pour the mixture into the pie plate and jiggle it back and forth gently to even it out.

3 Allow the mixture to begin to harden—only a few minutes! The mixture will begin to harden fast, usually within 6-10 minutes.

4 Place buttons gently on the surface of the still wet plaster. Very gently press them into the surface of the plaster.

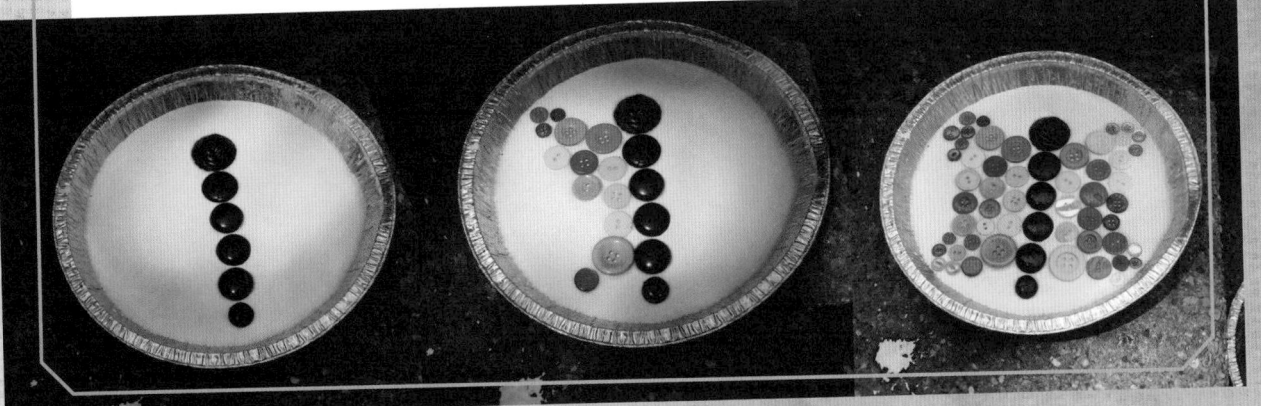

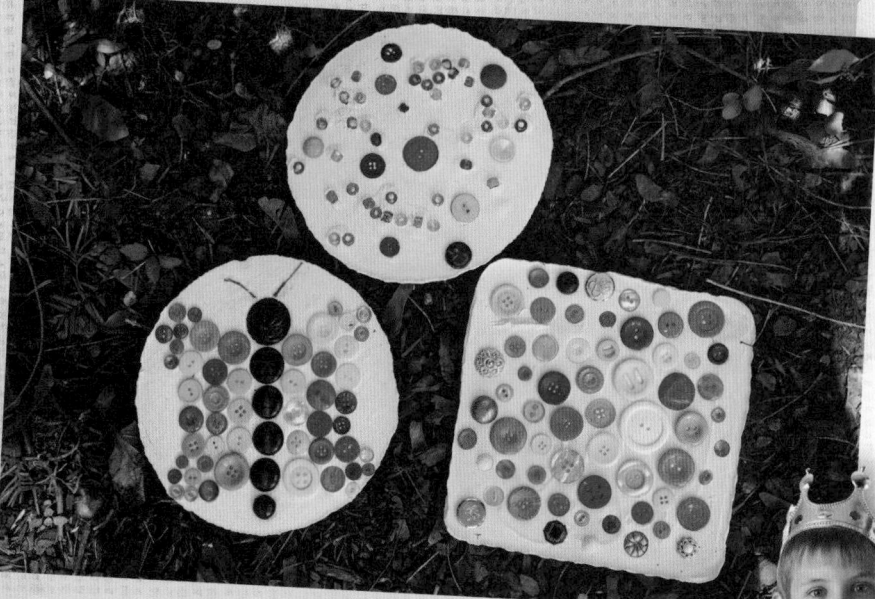

5 Allow the plaster to dry for several hours.

6 Remove the stones from the pan and carefully break off any jagged edges.

7 Dust off with a dry paintbrush then apply two coats of gloss sealer.

8 Your garden stones are ready to add color and flair to any garden!

ON THE BUTTON

King Francis I of France wore a court costume that had 13,600 golden buttons.

stuff For Noise

What You Need:

- ✓ 26 bottle caps
- ✓ Wide mouth canning band
- ✓ Hammer and nail
- ✓ 24 inches of braiding cord (available in the craft aisle)
- ✓ Hot glue gun

Inside-Out Maraca

Shake, shake, shake your inside-out maraca! With this project, you can see what you are shaking and what makes the sounds.

1 Flatten all the bottle caps and poke a hole in the center of each one (see pages 8-9).

2 Use the hammer and nail to poke a hole on each side of the canning band.

3 Thread the braiding cord through one of the holes in the canning band and wrap 5-6 inches of excess cord around the band and secure with hot glue.

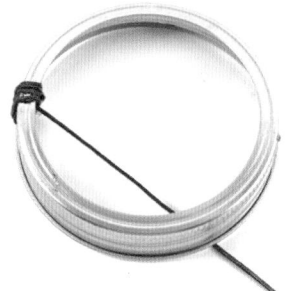

4 Thread the cord through the center of all of the bottle caps.

5 Slide all the caps to the end of the cord, then thread the cord through the second hole in the canning band.

6 Pull the cord tight and wrap the excess around the band, securing with hot glue.

7 Shake, shake, shake!

Monster Castanets

Clickity-clack! Clickity-clack! The monsters, they are coming back! Make this set of lovable monster head castanets using cardboard and bottle tops. Here's how.

What You Need:

✓ 2 cardboard rectangles, approximately 5" x 2"

✓ Paint

✓ 4 bottle caps

✓ White craft glue

✓ White paper

✓ Googly eyes

✓ Black marker (optional)

1 Fold each piece of cardboard in half and crease.

2 Paint the cardboard in the color of your choice.

3 When the paint is dry, glue a bottle cap to the inside of the cardboard, about ½ inch from one edge.

4 Cut teeth out of the white paper and glue to the other edge.

5 Glue a second bottle cap over the teeth. Position it so that when you bend the cardboard, the bottle caps tap together.

6 When dry, glue googly eyes to the front of the cardboard. A black marker is great for adding eyebrows.

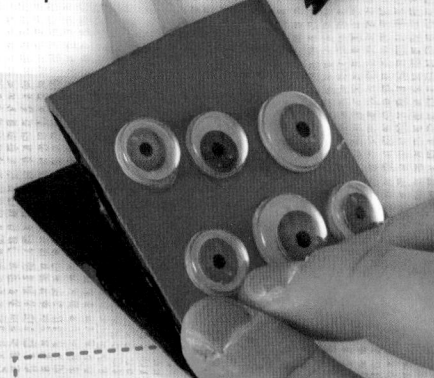

7 Clack, clack, clack!

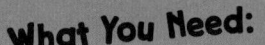

What You Need:

- ✓ 2 sturdy paper plates
- ✓ Hole puncher
- ✓ Hot glue gun
- ✓ 20 bottle caps
- ✓ Hammer and nail
- ✓ 30 inches of braiding cord, cut into 6-inch pieces
- ✓ 30 inches of ribbon or shoelace, cut into 6-inch pieces

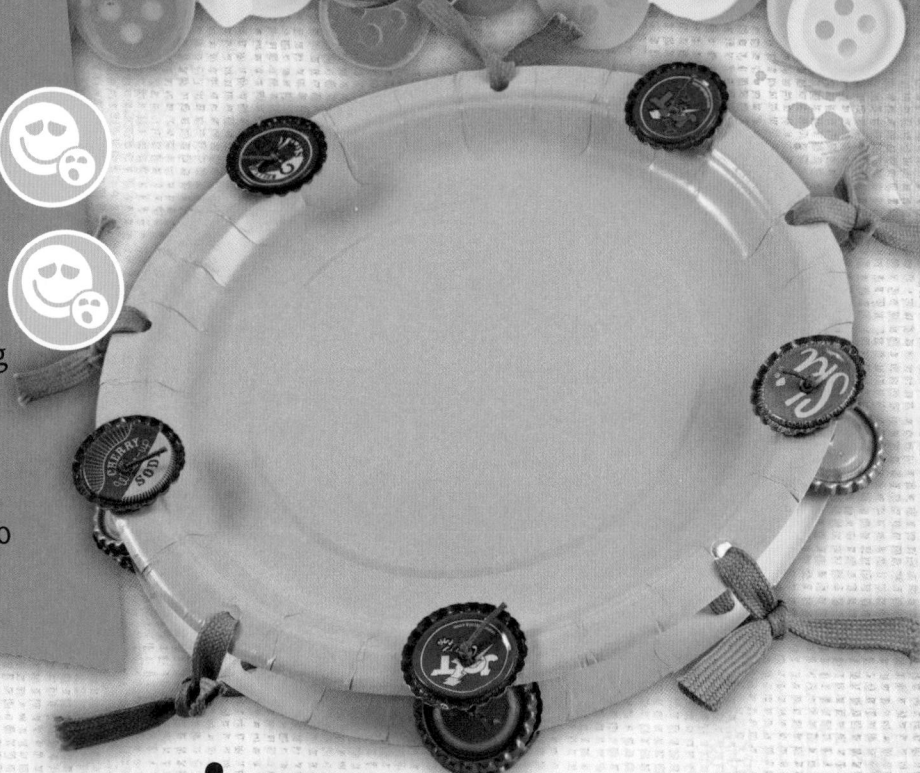

Tambourine

Making your own instruments is always fun, and this tambourine will be a big hit! Pair it with your maraca and mini-shakers for a rockin' good time!

1 Stack the two plates, front sides together, and use the hole puncher to make ten holes evenly spaced around the rim of both plates.

2 Turn the plates over so that the bottoms of the plates are touching each other and line up the holes. Glue the plates together.

3 Flatten each bottle cap and poke a hole through each center (see pages 8-9).

4 Tie a knot at one end of a piece of cord and thread the other end through a bottle cap.

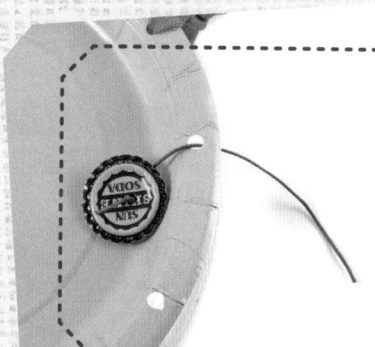

5 Thread the cord through one of the plate holes.

6 Add two more bottle caps to the cord and thread the cord through the second paper plate hole.

7 Add a fourth bottle cap to the cord and tie the cord in a knot. You should now have one cap on the outside of each plate and two caps between the two plates.

8 Hot glue the two outer bottle caps to the plates.

9 Repeat steps 4-8 at every other hole going around the plates.

10 Thread ribbon or shoelace through the holes you skipped in the plates and tie in a knot. Don't tie so tight that you bend the plates.

11 Find a beat and shake away!

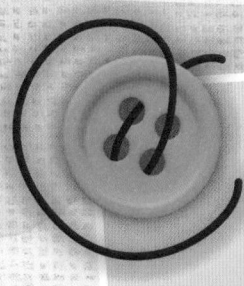

ON THE BUTTON

King Louis XIV of France is said to have spent $600,000 on jeweled buttons in one year.

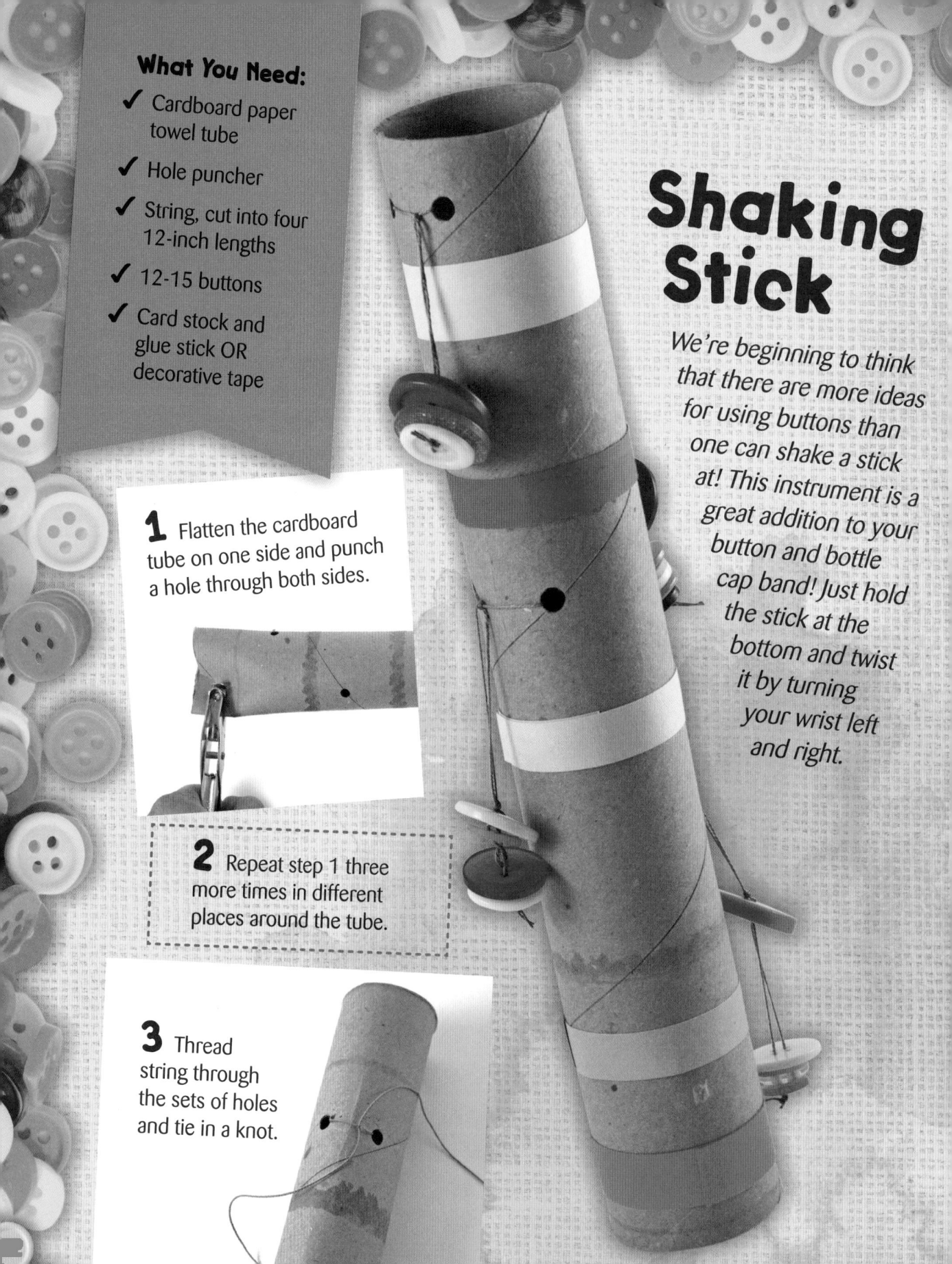

Shaking Stick

What You Need:

- ✓ Cardboard paper towel tube
- ✓ Hole puncher
- ✓ String, cut into four 12-inch lengths
- ✓ 12-15 buttons
- ✓ Card stock and glue stick OR decorative tape

We're beginning to think that there are more ideas for using buttons than one can shake a stick at! This instrument is a great addition to your button and bottle cap band! Just hold the stick at the bottom and twist it by turning your wrist left and right.

1 Flatten the cardboard tube on one side and punch a hole through both sides.

2 Repeat step 1 three more times in different places around the tube.

3 Thread string through the sets of holes and tie in a knot.

4 Tie a second knot in each length of string, about two inches from the edge of the tube.

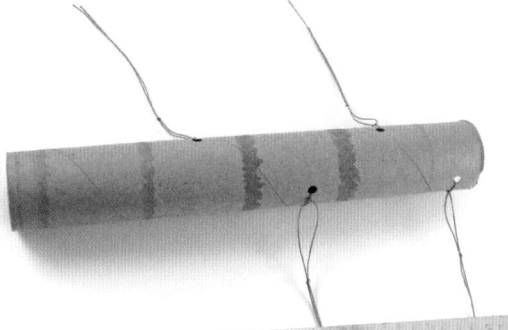

5 Thread buttons onto the strings up to the knots. Tie another knot to secure them.

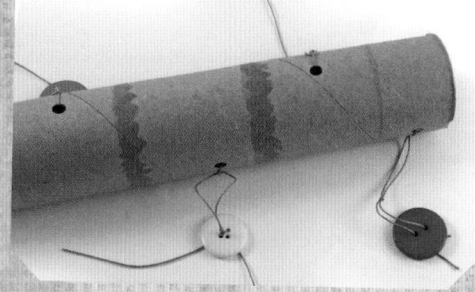

6 Add one or two more buttons to each string.

7 Decorate your tube with strips of card stock and a glue stick, or decorative tape.

8 Twist and shout!

Mini-Shaker

These mini-shakers are like teeny tiny maracas without a handle! A fun and musical way to recycle those plastic bottle caps. Get shakin'!

What You Need:
- ✔ 2 equal-sized plastic bottle caps
- ✔ Small beads
- ✔ Duct tape

1 Pour some beads inside of one of the bottle caps.

2 Place the second lid on top of the first, open ends touching.

3 Tape the lids shut with duct tape.

4 Shake, rattle, and roll!

stuff to Hang

What You Need:

✓ Measuring tape

✓ String

✓ Scissors

✓ White craft glue

✓ Parchment paper or wax paper

✓ Lots and lots of buttons

✓ Felt

✓ Hot glue gun

✓ Spring tension curtain rod

Button Curtain

Whether you choose a colorful rainbow theme or your favorite team colors, this is a great way to add some personal style to your room, and looks awesome hanging in a window or a doorway. This project can take a full afternoon, making it a fun project to do with a friend, at camp, or during a sleepover!

1 Measure the length of the doorway or window you plan to decorate and add 12 inches.

2 Decide how many button strands you want to hang. You can space them close together, or farther apart. Cut enough pieces of string, at the length you measured in step 1, to space across your window or door.

3 Cover your work surface with parchment or wax paper.

4 Lay a string across the parchment paper. Beginning about six inches from the top of the string, place one button under the string. Add a generous amount of glue over the string and button.

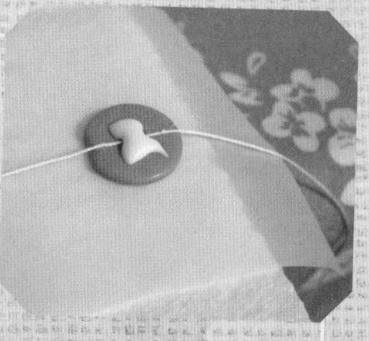

5 Place a second, similarly sized button, on top of the glue, sandwiching the string between the two buttons.

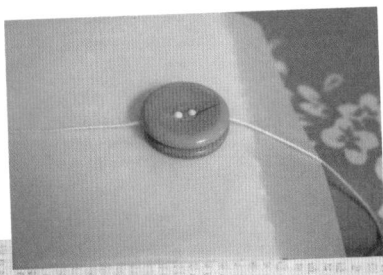

6 Repeat steps 4-5 until you've reached the desired length.

7 Make as many strands as you want.

8 To hang each strand, cut two equal-sized strips of felt, about 5" x 1". Place one strip of felt on the table and lay the top of a strand over the felt.

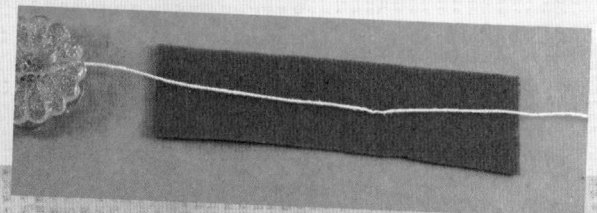

9 Line the second strip of felt with hot glue and place on top of the first one, sandwiching the string between the strips. Trim off the excess string.

10 Add some hot glue to the end of the felt closest to the buttons.

11 Fold the top of the felt strip down onto the glue to create a loop.

12 Repeat steps 8-11 for each button strand.

13 To hang, string the loops onto the curtain rod.

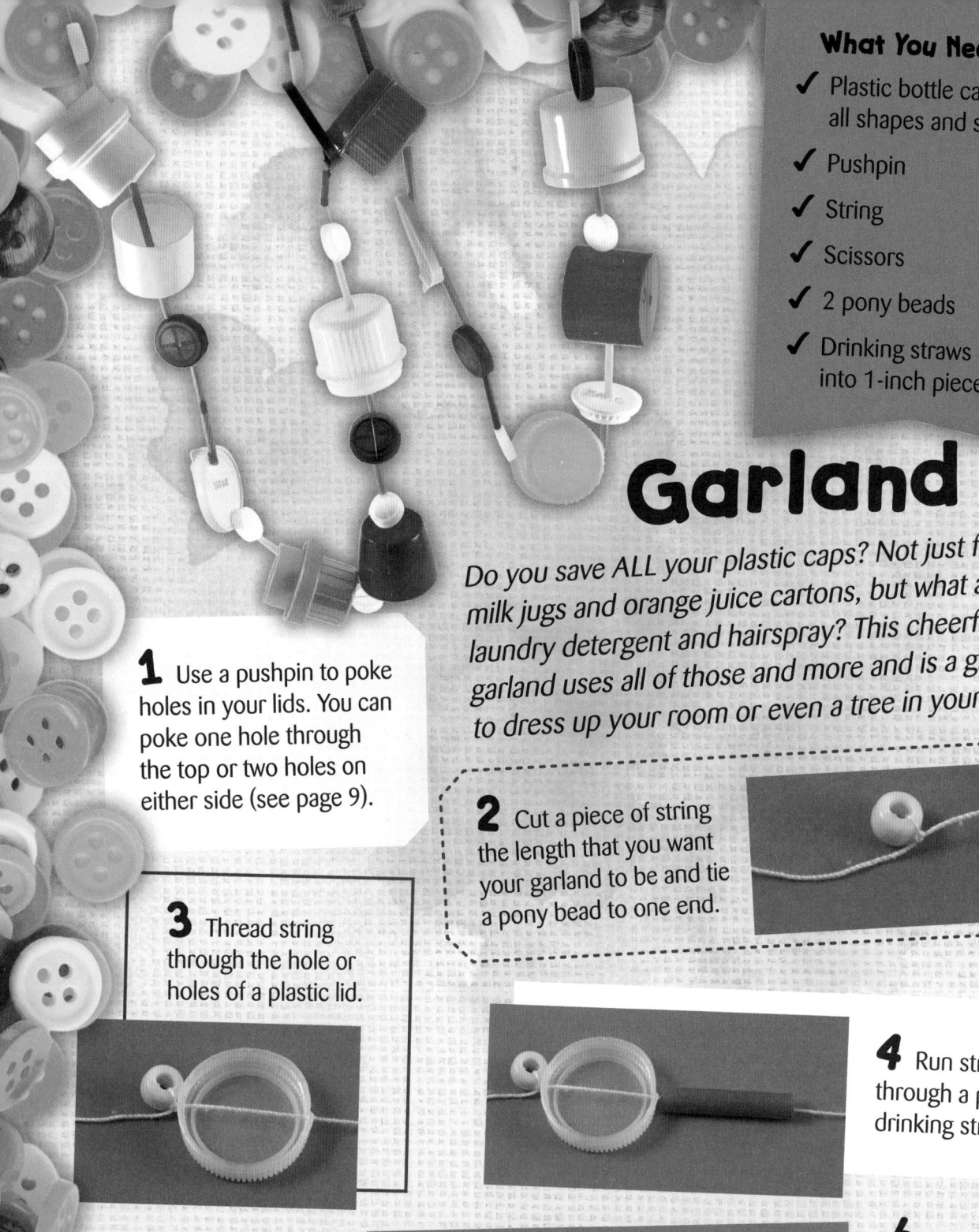

What You Need:

✓ Plastic bottle caps of all shapes and sizes

✓ Pushpin

✓ String

✓ Scissors

✓ 2 pony beads

✓ Drinking straws (cut into 1-inch pieces)

Garland

Do you save ALL your plastic caps? Not just from milk jugs and orange juice cartons, but what about laundry detergent and hairspray? This cheerful garland uses all of those and more and is a great way to dress up your room or even a tree in your yard!

1 Use a pushpin to poke holes in your lids. You can poke one hole through the top or two holes on either side (see page 9).

2 Cut a piece of string the length that you want your garland to be and tie a pony bead to one end.

3 Thread string through the hole or holes of a plastic lid.

4 Run string through a piece of drinking straw.

5 Repeat steps 3-4 until you are happy with the length of your garland.

6 Tie a pony bead to the end of the garland to hold all of the caps and straw pieces in place.

What You Need:

- ✓ 18-inch piece of twine or cord
- ✓ 3 medium brown buttons
- ✓ 10-12 green (or various colors) buttons varying in size from large to small
- ✓ Star bead or small pony bead

Button Ornament

Stacking buttons is an easy way to create fun ornaments. Try this tree or get creative and make up your own designs! All you need is a handful of buttons and some cord.

1 Before you begin, make sure that your cord or twine will go through the holes of your smallest button. If you don't do this test, you could get all the way to the end and not be able to add the last piece!

2 Thread the cord through a hole in one of the medium brown buttons.

3 Thread the other end of the cord through a second hole in the button and pull the cord taut, making sure that the ends of the cord line up evenly.

4 Add the other two brown buttons in the same fashion.

5 Now add the largest green button. Continue adding buttons, largest to smallest, until all buttons have been added.

6 Thread both ends of cord through the star bead or pony bead and tie in a knot.

7 Tie the ends of the cord together to create a hanger.

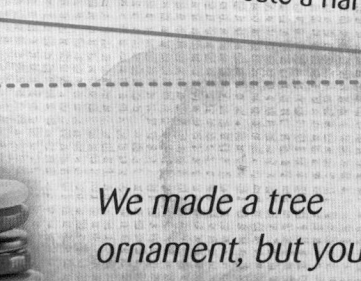

We made a tree ornament, but you can make up a design of your own!

Button Snowman

You can easily make little snowmen from buttons that are great for adding to homemade greeting cards, attaching to the top of a gift, making into a magnet, or attaching some ribbon to make an ornament!

1 Glue three buttons in the shape of a snowman to a piece of felt.

2 Cut around the buttons to create a snowman.

3 Add a little glue between the buttons to keep the snowman from bending.

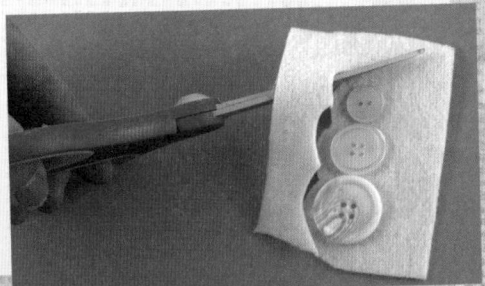

5 Cut a simple top hat from black felt and glue to the top button.

4 Cut a strip of felt for a scarf and glue between the top and middle buttons.

6 Cut about ½ inch from the tip of an orange toothpick and glue to the top button.

TOP TIP: If you don't have orange toothpicks, you can use paint or a marker to color a plain one.

What You Need:

- ✓ Clear plastic lid
- ✓ Needle and string or thread
- ✓ White craft glue
- ✓ Paintbrush
- ✓ Translucent beads

Sun Catcher

Here comes the sun! Catch the rays by making these easy sun catchers from plastic lids and colorful beads.

1 Thread the needle and poke it through the side rim of the plastic lid.

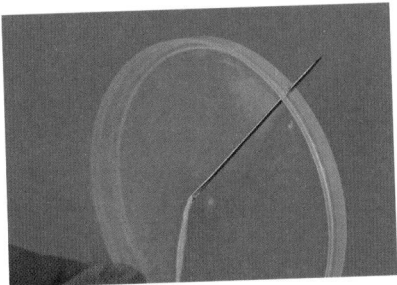

2 Pull the thread through and tie in a knot.

3 Squeeze about a teaspoon of white glue into the plastic lid and spread it around with a paintbrush.

4 While glue is still wet place beads in the plastic lid and allow it to dry several hours or overnight.

5 Hang in a window!

stuff for fun

Button Animals

What You Need:
- ✓ Buttons in various sizes and colors
- ✓ Hot glue
- ✓ Googly eyes
- ✓ Card stock

How many different animals do you think you can make from buttons? How about a frog? Or a penguin? What about a bear? See how many different animals you can make. Put together an entire button zoo!

1 Use larger buttons for the body and smaller buttons for the head and any other parts like legs or ears.

2 Hot glue buttons together.

3 Glue on googly eyes.

4 Cut beaks, wings, or fins from card stock and glue to your animals.

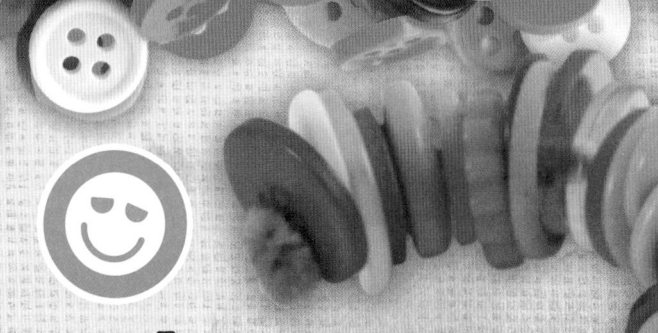

Inchworm

*So cute, and it couldn't be easier!
Pull out your button stash and a pipe
cleaner to make this colorful inchworm.*

1 Poke the pipe cleaner through a hole in a button and slide the button down to the end of the pipe cleaner. Bend the bottom end to secure.

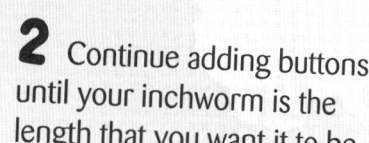

2 Continue adding buttons until your inchworm is the length that you want it to be.

3 Trim the excess pipe cleaner and bend it to secure.

4 Glue googly eyes onto one end.

READY TO MAKE ONE OF THE SIMPLEST TOYS EVER?

Thread a piece of string (about two feet long) through one hole in a button and back through another hole. Tie a knot in the string to make a big loop. Slide the button to the middle of the string and hold the string with one hand at each end. Swing the button around in a circle to wind up the string a bunch of times. Now pull your hands out a bit. The button will begin to spin! Move your hands in and out to keep it spinning. Presto! You made a button top!

Floppy Horse

Who knew that bottle caps could be transformed into a floppy toy? We made a horse, but with a little imagination you can make a giraffe, a clown, a bear—it's up to you! Using a light floral wire allows your toy to flop around, just like an old rag doll.

What You Need:

✓ 122 bottle caps, holes poked into the center of each (see page 9)

✓ 24-gauge floral wire

✓ Wire cutters

✓ 4 large shank buttons

✓ 5 medium buttons

✓ 8-10 twist ties

✓ Cork

✓ Toothpick

✓ Scissors

✓ Hot glue gun

✓ Flat nose pliers (optional)

✓ 2 small buttons (eyes)

1 Cut four pieces of wire, 16 inches each.

2 Thread a large button onto one of the wires, center it in the middle of the wire, and twist the wire once or twice to secure.

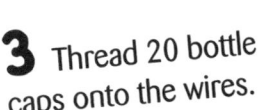

3 Thread 20 bottle caps onto the wires.

4 Thread the ends of the wires through a medium button and twist the wire a couple times to secure.

5 Repeat steps 2-4 for the three remaining legs. Set the legs aside.

6 Cut a length of wire 24 inches long and fold it in half.

7 Gather four twist ties and twist together in the center two times.

8 Place the center of the twist ties in the center of the wire. Twist the wire around the ties to secure.

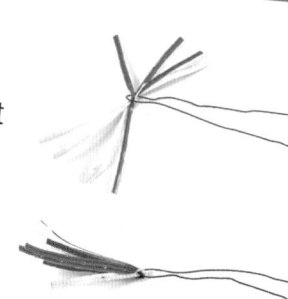

9 To create the body, thread 42 bottle caps onto the wires. Set aside.

10 To create the head, use a toothpick to make a hole through the cork. Using pliers to grasp, push, and pull the toothpick is helpful.

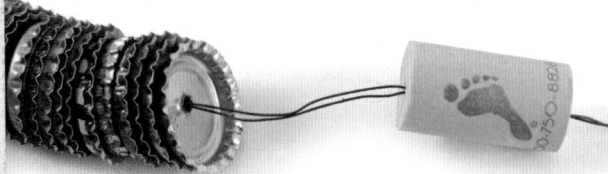

11 Thread the ends of the body wire through the cork and then thread on a medium button. Twist the wire a few times and snip off the excess.

12 Attach two legs to the back of the body by inserting the end of the wire between two bottle caps near the tail. Wrap the wire around a few times and snip off the excess.

13 Attach two front legs toward the front of the body.

14 To create the mane, cut the remaining twist ties in half and wrap them around the wire between bottle caps on the neck.

15 Hot glue the two small buttons to the sides of the cork for eyes.

TOP TIP #1: Pipe cleaners can be substituted for twist ties.

TOP TIP #2: If you don't want your toy to be quite so floppy, use heavier wire.

Button Man

This little man is as cute as a button! You can use dark buttons for the legs to look like pants, and even make flared jeans by using larger buttons at the bottom and adding smaller buttons as you work your way up!

1 Fold each piece of wire in half and thread a small round bead onto one end.

2 Twist the wire a few times to secure the bead. Repeat for the second wire.

4 Twist the wire a few times at the end of the last button. Then twist both wires together to connect the legs.

3 To make the legs, thread buttons onto the wire, putting each wire through a separate buttonhole. Add as many as you like; we used 15 for each leg.

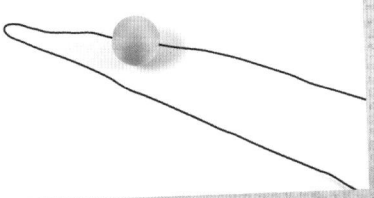

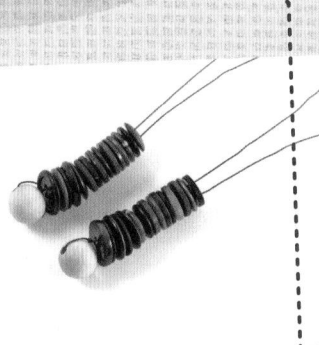

5 Separate the wires, two on the left and two on the right. Thread buttons onto the wires. Add as many as you like; we used 11.

6 Separate the wires again. Bend one to the left, one right, and two stay straight.

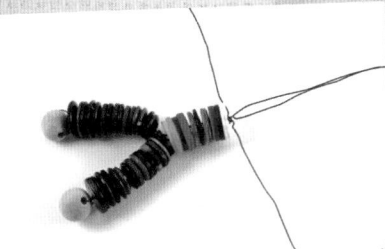

7 Add two buttons and the large round bead to the two straight wires.

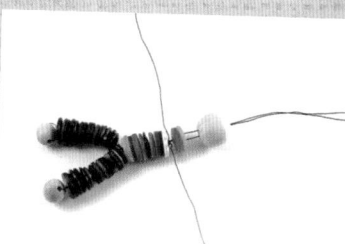

8 Take the wires from the top of the bead and thread them back down through the two buttons below. Do this on both sides of the bead and pull the wire all the way through.

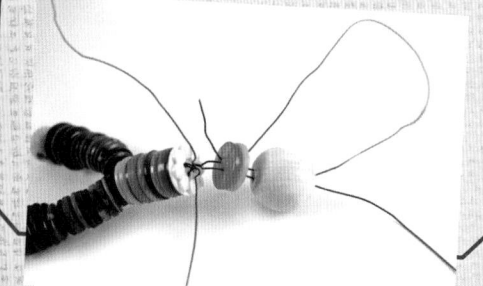

9 You will now have two wires on the left and two on the right.

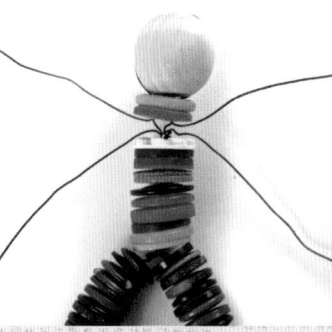

10 Thread buttons onto the wires for the arms; we used 15 on each.

11 Thread the arm wires through a small round wooden bead.

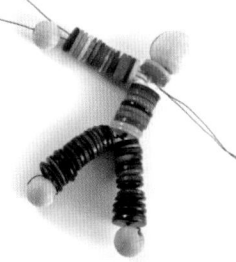

12 Wrap the wire around the bead and back through the hole again. Pull the wires tight.

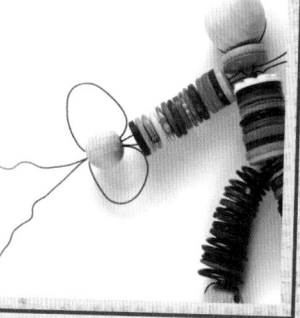

13 Use wire cutters to snip off all but one inch, then twist the excess and tuck it into the bead opening. Pliers are helpful in this step.

14 Say hello to Button Man!

Bottle Cap Bugs

What You Need:
- ✓ Plastic bottle caps
- ✓ Black marker or black paint
- ✓ Googly eyes
- ✓ White craft glue
- ✓ Scissors
- ✓ Pipe cleaners

Plastic bottle caps are the perfect shape for making ladybugs and other insects! Decorate them however you like and give them their own little personalities.

1 Draw or paint dots or stripes onto your plastic caps.

2 Glue on googly eyes.

3 If adding wings, cut a small plastic cap in half and glue to the top of the bug.

4 For legs, cut a pipe cleaner into pieces and glue to the underside of the plastic lid, then bend into shape. You might want to cut a small circle of paper to glue in place over the pipe cleaners on the underside.

stuff to create

Monogram

Use bunches of colorful buttons to personalize just about anything! You can add a letter monogram to the lid of a small box like we did, or make a monogram to go inside a picture frame to hang on your wall.

What You Need:
- ✓ Colorful buttons
- ✓ Scrap paper and pencil
- ✓ White craft glue
- ✓ Surface to personalize (canvas, box, frame, etc)

1 Use a piece of scrap paper to sketch your letter and lay out the buttons.

3 Transfer buttons, one at a time, from your scrap paper to the glue on your project surface.

2 Once you have your design ready, use white glue to draw your letter on your project surface.

4 Allow the glue to dry completely.

Embroidery Hoop Wall Art

What You Need:

- ✓ Embroidery hoop
- ✓ Scissors
- ✓ Fabric
- ✓ 7 large buttons
- ✓ 7 small buttons
- ✓ Green and white embroidery thread
- ✓ Needle
- ✓ Hot glue gun

If you can sew on a button, you can make this beautiful piece of wall art for your room! Who knew?

1 Cut your fabric so it is a few inches larger than your embroidery hoop.

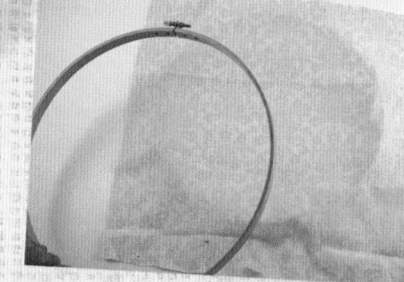

2 Separate the hoop and place the inner hoop underneath the fabric.

3 Place the outer hoop over the top of the fabric and push down to sandwich the fabric between the two hoops, then tighten the hoop with the top screw.

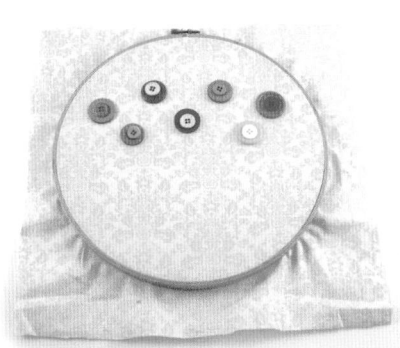

4 Before you do any sewing, place your buttons on the fabric to decide where you want them. We are layering small buttons on top of large buttons.

5 Sew the large buttons onto the fabric with white thread (see page 6).

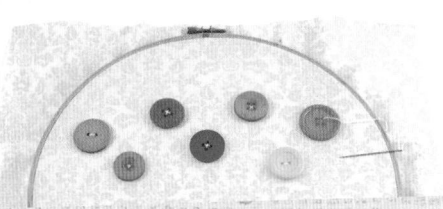

6 Sew the smaller buttons over the top of the larger buttons, going through the holes of the large buttons as well.

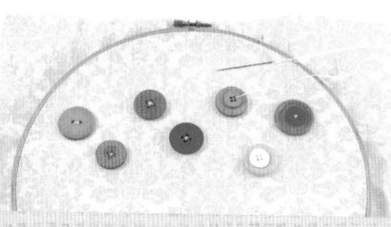

7 Sew a stem with green thread using a running stitch (see page 7). Repeat for all stems. Tie off thread in the back.

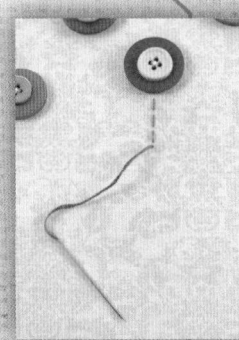

8 Trim off excess fabric around the hoop, leaving about a ½-inch border.

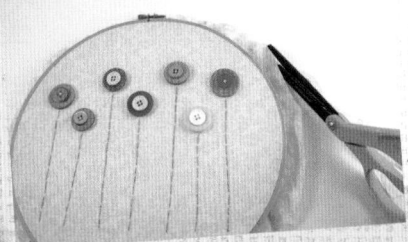

9 Turn the hoop over and glue the excess fabric to the back of the hoop.

TOP TIP: Embroidery thread is made up of six individual strands. We used two strands of each color for this craft.

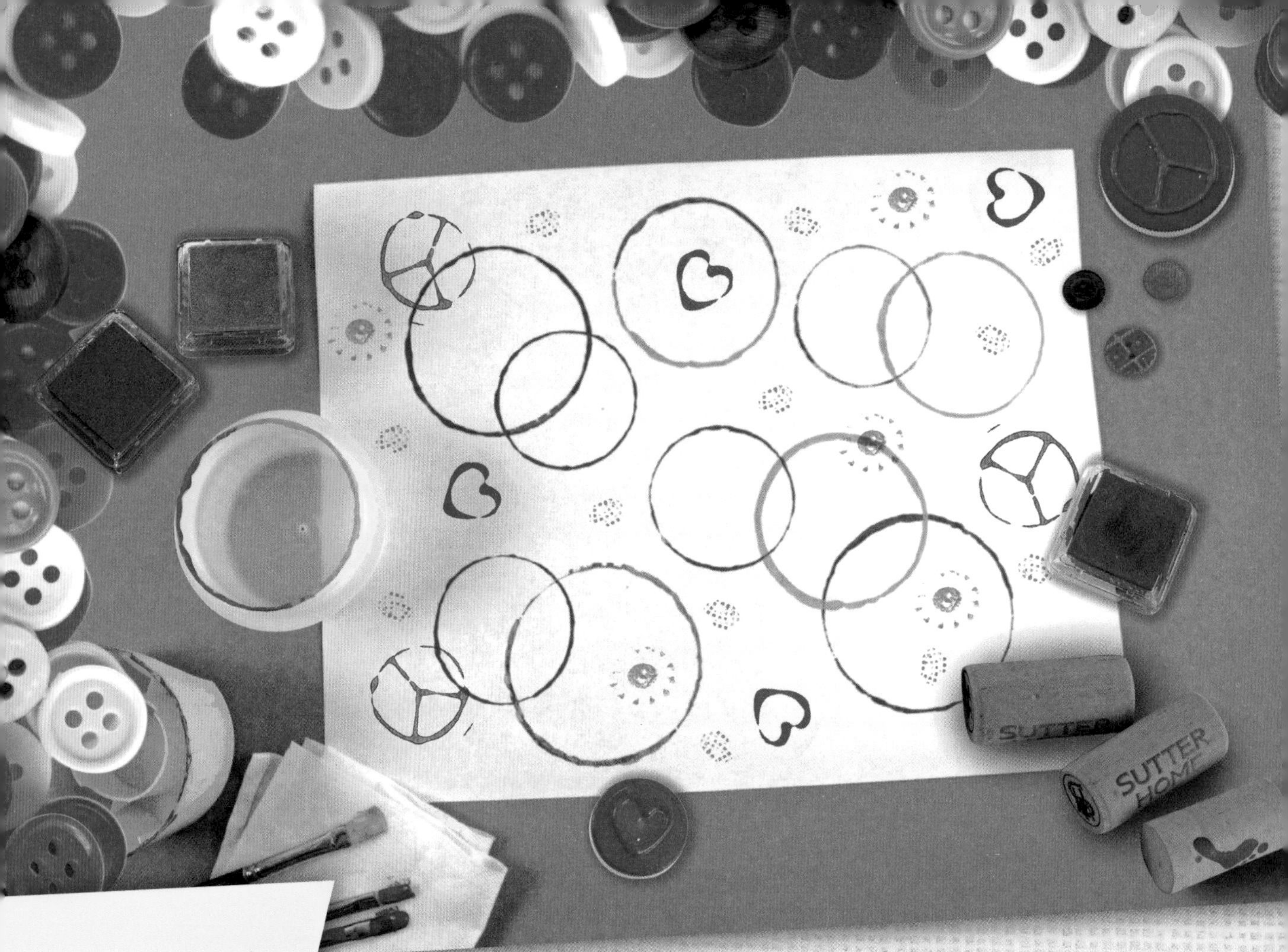

What You Need:

- ✓ Tall lids or caps
- ✓ Paper
- ✓ Craft paint
- ✓ Paintbrushes

Cap Stamp Art

Plastic caps are the perfect materials to create your own simple circle stamps. Design an abstract painting or use the caps to make a face or the wheels of a vehicle.

1 Use a paintbrush to paint the edge of a lid.

2 Press the painted end onto the paper.

3 Lift straight up.

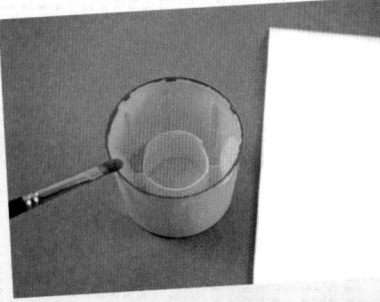

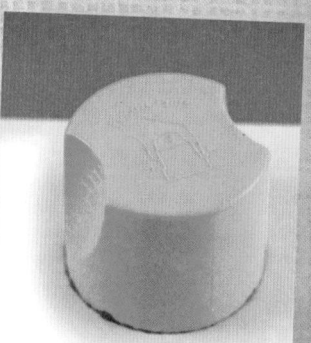

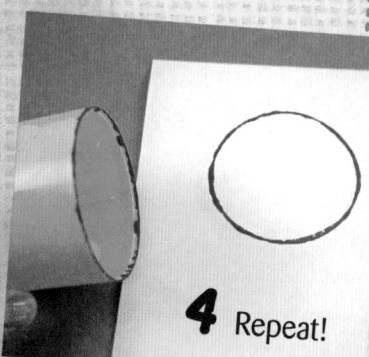

4 Repeat!

Button Stamp

Stamps are great for decorating wrapping paper, or making your own stationery or note cards. Make your own unique designs with textured buttons and corks. You can buy bags of corks at the craft store!

1 Hot glue each button to the end of a cork.

2 Press the button end of the cork stamp into the inked stamp pad.

3 Press onto paper. Depending on your button, you may need to roll the button on the paper. Rocking it back and forth creates interesting designs as well.

TOP TIP: If you are using a shank button, press the shank of the button into the cork to create a hole, then glue the button in place.

Bottle Cap Stamp

Here's another great way to make your own stamps. All you need is a few milk jug and water bottle caps and some puffy paint! A little patience is needed for the puffy paint to dry, but then you can use your stamps over and over again.

1 Use puffy paint to draw simple designs or write words or numbers on the flat side of the plastic lid.

3 Press the stamp into the stamp pad and onto your paper to create designs.

2 Allow puffy paint to dry overnight.

What You Need:

- ✓ Plastic caps of various sizes and colors
- ✓ Foam core board
- ✓ White craft glue

Bottle Cap Mosaic

Find your inner Picasso! Here's a fun way to use up a bunch of plastic caps and lids that you have all over the house—create some awesome visual art for your room! We've made ours in rainbow colors, but you can choose whatever colors you like.

1 Group your plastic lids by color.

2 Begin in one area of the foam core and glue lids of one color closely together, covering as much of the board as you want.

3 Continue with each color, one at a time, as you work across the board.

4 Fill any empty space with white or clear lids.

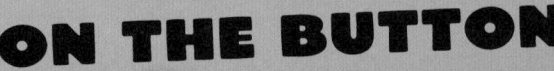

ON THE BUTTON

According to Guiness World Records, the largest button mosaic measured over 4,224 square feet and was made by Fareed Lafta in Dubai, in March 2013. It featured 1,019,078 buttons!

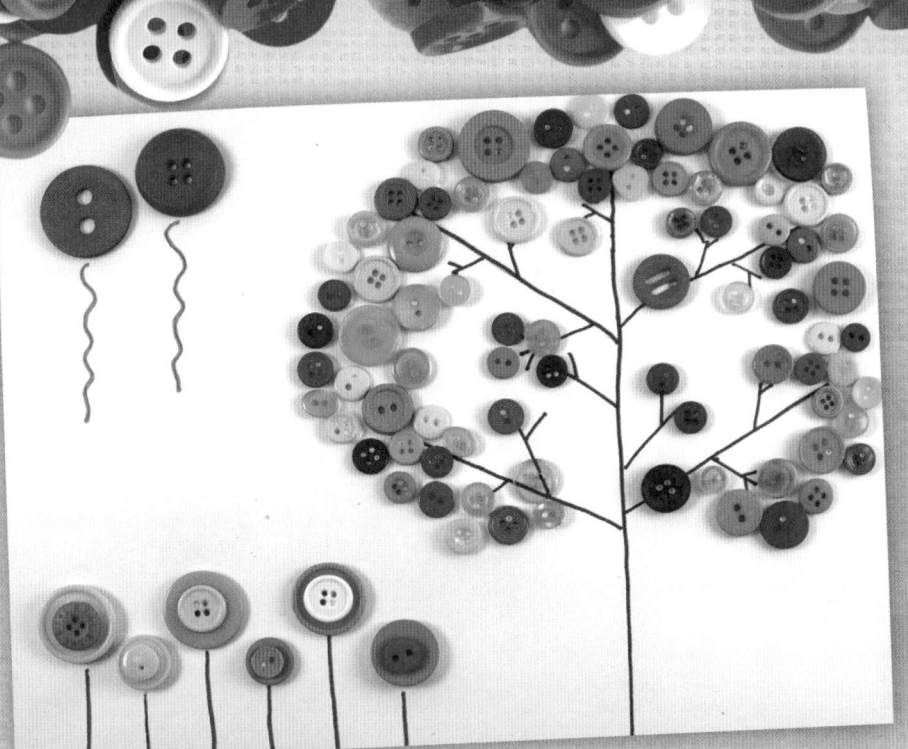

Button Collage

Use buttons to create a fun collage! Here we've used buttons as flowers, balloons, and leaves on a tree. Use your imagination to create your own colorful collage.

1 Use a pencil to draw the basic lines of your picture.

2 Use markers to trace over your pencil lines.

3 Use white glue to attach buttons to your card stock, creating your collage.

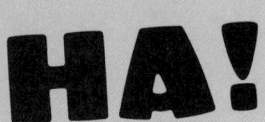

HA!

Q. What did the policeman say to his belly button?

A. You're under a vest.

stuff for Home

Lampshade

This cheerful lampshade can make your room as bright as a button! Grab your button stash and a hot glue gun and in about twenty minutes you'll have an entirely new lamp.

What You Need:

✓ Lamp with fabric shade

✓ Lots of buttons in a variety of sizes and colors

✓ Hot glue gun

1 Take the shade off the lamp.

2 Apply a dot of hot glue directly to the shade.

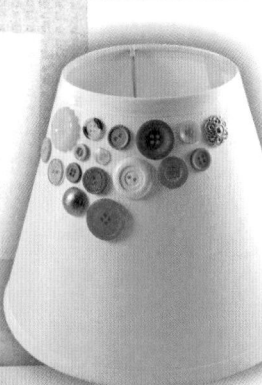

3 Select a button and press it in place on the shade.

4 Keep adding buttons until you have covered your whole shade!

TOP TIP: If you don't have enough buttons to cover the whole shade, you can just add button borders to the top and bottom rims of your shade.

Button Tree

This pretty button tree can be made in a rainbow of colors, or choose a single color to go with a room's décor. Try orange and black buttons for a spooky Halloween tree. Or red and green for a great Christmas decoration!

1 Thread a piece of wire up through each button and back down again.

2 Pull the wire tight and twist both ends together.

3 Line up all the button "branches" and twist the ends together.

4 Insert the twisted end into the center of the spool so your tree will stand up.

5 Separate the branches into groups of three.

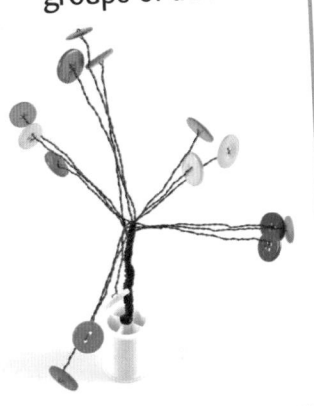

6 Now twist each set of three branches halfway to the buttons.

7 Move the branches around until your tree looks the way you want it to!

Button Bouquet

No glue, no tape, nothing sticky needed! This pretty bouquet of button flowers would be great for Mother's Day or just for dressing up a potted plant. Make five or fifty, the more the merrier!

What You Need (for each flower):

✓ 4 buttons (small to large in graduated sizes)

✓ 24-gauge floral wire, 16 inches in length

1 Thread wire through one hole in each button, starting with the largest size and working your way to the smallest.

2 Run the wire back down through all four buttons.

3 Pull the wire tight and twist it to secure the buttons in place and create a stem.

4 Now that you see how easy it is, make another. And another!

What You Need:

- ✓ Paper clip
- ✓ 2 buttons of similar size
- ✓ Hot glue gun

Bookmark

Sure you can dog-ear a page to save your place, but imagine how much fun you can have marking your books with these simple, adorable bookmarks. So easy to make, you'll want to create some for friends, family, and your teacher!

1 Add some hot glue to the back of one of the buttons.

2 Press the end of the paper clip into the hot glue.

3 Before the glue begins to dry, press the second button over the top, sandwiching the paper clip in between the two buttons.

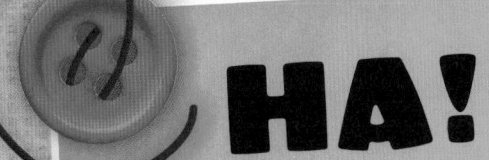

HA!

Q. Round as a button,
Deep as a well.
If you want me to talk,
You must first pull my tail.
What am I?

A. A bell.

Bottle Cap Emoticons

LOL! Express yourself with these simple magnets made from recycled plastic bottle caps.

What You Need:

✓ 1 plastic milk jug cap

✓ 1 plastic water bottle cap

✓ Hot glue gun

✓ Magnet

✓ 2 googly eyes

✓ White puffy paint

1 Turn the milk jug cap upside down and use hot glue to attach the water bottle cap, flat side facing out.

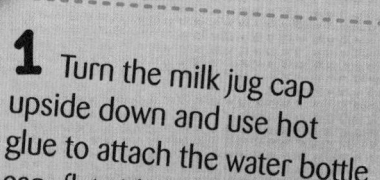

2 Glue a magnet to the water bottle lid.

3 Glue googly eyes to the front side of the milk jug cap.

Here are some ideas:

:) SMILE

:D BIG GRIN

:O SURPRISED

:/ PERPLEXED

:| BORED

:(SAD

4 Use white puffy paint to add a nose and mouth.

Bottle Cap Magnet

What you decide to put inside the bottle cap is completely up to you. You can make colorful polka dots like we did, or use a photo of you and your friends. Or cut out your initial and glue it in place. You are only limited by your imagination!

1 Cut a circle from the card stock to fit inside the bottle cap. You can trace the bottle cap onto the card stock and then cut it out and trim it to fit.

2 Glue the card stock circle to the inside of the bottle cap.

3 Use a toothpick dipped in white paint to add polka dots to the card stock.

4 Glue a magnet to the back of the bottle cap.

Button Thumbtack

Here's a great way to dress up that boring corkboard in your room! Use your favorite colorful buttons to hold all your stuff in place.

1 Glue the back of the button to the thumbtack and allow it to dry completely.

Soap Dish

What You Need:

- ✓ Large plastic lid, any shape
- ✓ 4 plastic milk jug caps
- ✓ White craft glue
- ✓ Pebbles (buy them at a craft store or find them outside)

This upcycling* project is a great way to make something out of "nothing." The finished product is pretty enough for your powder room sink!

1 Glue the milk jug lids to the large plastic lid, top-side-down.

2 Apply glue to the exposed areas of the lid.

3 Cover the glue with pebbles.

4 Shake off any loose pebbles and be sure all areas are covered.

5 Let dry for several hours before using.

*Upcycling is when you use waste materials to makes something useful. This book is packed with upcycling projects like this one!

Kitty Tote Bag

Looks like the cat's out of the bag! Well, it's on the outside of the bag anyway. This is a fun way to dress up an overnight tote bag, or book bag.

1 Thread the needle with two strands of embroidery thread, about 20 inches long. Decide where you would like the eyes to go.

2 Starting from the inside of the bag, sew on one of the green buttons (see page 6).

3 Sew on the second green button next to the first.

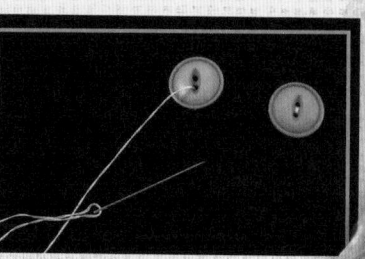

4 Sew on the pink button, between and below the two green buttons.

5 Tie off thread behind the pink button on the inside of the bag and trim excess thread.

6 Use more white thread to sew running stitches on both sides of the pink button for the whiskers (see page 7). Tie off each whisker with a small knot inside the bag.

TOP TIP: Don't have a black tote bag? Use a white one and black thread.

Amanda Formaro is a Midwest mother of four who has been creating crafts for kids for over 20 years. She has been published in several major magazines, including *Parents*, *Redbook*, and *Family Fun*, and websites including Family.com, and Spoonful.com. Her passion for crafting resonates in her blog, **CraftsbyAmanda.com**, where she shares tutorials with step-by-step photos for adults and kids alike. Amanda loves the creative process and trying new things, and especially likes making something from nothing.